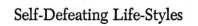

Self-Defeating Life-Styles

SELF-DEFEATING LIFE-STYLES

Christopher C. Conver
and
Leigh E. Conver

BROADMAN PRESS
Nashville, Tennessee

ISBN: 0-8054-5441-1
Dewey Decimal Classification: 158
Subject Heading: PSYCHOLOGY, APPLIED // LIFESTYLES
Library of Congress Catalog Card Number: 88-6518
Printed in the United States of America

Library of Congress Cataloging-in-Publication Data

Conver, Christopher C., 1956-
    Self-defeating lifestyles / by Christopher C. Conver and Leigh E. Conver.
    p. cm. — (The Bible and personal crisis)
    ISBN 0-8054-5441-1
    1. Christian life—1960-   2. Adjustment (Psychology)   3. Life style.
I. Conver, Leigh E., 1947-   . II Title.   III. Series.
BV4501.2.C67255   1988
248.4—dc19   88-6518
                                                    CIP

Acknowledgments

The authors would like to acknowledge several individuals who have been sojourners with them and in so doing have deepened and enriched our lives.

We are thankful and appreciative of our families. To Marion and Charles Conver, our parents, Lynn and Tan, our brothers, who were the nuclear family of our birth and our entrance into the body of Christ, we give our deepest appreciation and thanks.

To our wives, Patti and Linda, and our children—Benjamin, James, Samuel, Jonathan, and Leslie—we acknowledge the grace and forgiveness available throughout our professional lives and especially in the writing of this book, as time has been stolen from these cherished ones in order to pursue the yearning for knowledge.

To the many friends and colleagues, too numerous to name, whose encouragement has helped us to have courage in the writing when the temptation has been to falter, we offer our gratitude.

To the staff of the Pastoral Services Department of the Georgia Baptist Medical Center and of the Baptist Book Store at The Southern Baptist Theological Seminary, we express our appreciation for allowing us time to research and reflect upon this task.

To Dr. Edward Thornton and Dr. Gerald Borchart, who guided our individual graduate programs, we will always be grateful for their wisdom, inspiration, and patience. It is a singular joy to be sharing in this collection as coauthors with these two talented men of God.

To Broadman Press we are grateful for the opportunity to work together in this undertaking and to give back to our denomination some portion of the knowledge which Southern Baptists through the Cooperative Program have enabled us to achieve.

And to the many counselees, students, and parishioners—saints and fellow pilgrims all—who have shared their personal life stories in the task of overcoming their unique patterns of self-defeating behaviors, this book is dedicated with our deepest gratitude and appreciation.

LEIGH E. CONVER, Ph.D.
Atlanta, Georgia

CHRISTOPHER C. CONVER, Ph.D.
Louisville, Kentucky

Contents

Introduction

People try to cope with stress, fears, and anxiety daily. Stress stems from pressures at work or school or in the family. Fears bother us from infancy to death, forcing us to redirect our lives to avoid them. Anxiety gnaws at us in our quiet or reflective moments, confirming for us the hopelessness of our present predicament. How a person deals with stress, fears, and anxiety is a factor in determining what type of life-style that person leads. For most, a normal life-style, full of healthy outlets to cope, is chosen. For some, though, a self-defeating life-style, through a distortion of a healthy outlet, is chosen.

In writing this book, we have merged our individual specialities of New Testament scholarship and pastoral counseling to provide an introduction to the problem of self-defeating life-styles. Each of twelve different life-styles is presented by both a case study of how this life-style might be encountered in today's society and an accompanying biblical narrative and/or word study. Each life-style is interpreted through two lenses—a biblical lens and a psychological lens. Our intent is to show how each of these life-styles are distortions of healthy strategies to respond to stressful, fearful, or anxiety-filled challenges of life. The strategies themselves are not self-defeating; rather, the

9

overdevelopment of an aspect of each strategy leads to a self-defeating life-style. We hope this book offers some suggestions Christians can use to modify these life-style strategies to avoid their potentially self-defeating outcomes.

When God created Adam in Genesis 1 and before the entrance of sin into his life, Adam had the full measure of the creative potential of how humans were to be. Adam had the fullness of creative personhood. The manner in which Adam lived was intended to be the manner in which all humans could live.

The biblical record concerning Adam gives us a picture of creative personhood. Humans were created in God's image (Gen. 1:27), blessed (Gen. 1:28), and declared good (Gen. 1:31). The natural or inherent aspects of humanity, taken in the proper context, are normal and good. Emotions, relationships with others, and self-respect are natural, healthy, and within God's intentions for every person. To feel anger or shame, to love or admire someone else, or to take pride in one's own strengths are feelings each of us should have. The overemphasis of some of these feelings coupled with a detrimental defense mechanism, though, can hinder the image of God within each of us. The sinful union of overemphasized feelings and detrimental defense mechanisms is what leads to a self-defeating life-style.

Fortunately most of us do not live in isolation. Unfortunately the detrimental aspects of our personalities have links to the personalities of those with whom we are in community. The self-defeating life-styles of an individual affects the members of his or her family too. To offer any resolution for an individual problem frequently requires offering assistance for the shared family problem as well. The presence of a self-defeating life-style in one member of the family may suggest the possibility of a life-style problem in another member too.

When the Word became flesh, as related in John 1:1, God not only gave the world His perfect Child but gave us a representative of redeemed humanity also. The ways in which Jesus encountered and dealt with the challenges of life show us that God responds in grace to human sin and that same divine response is also the means to overcome sin. The redemptive responses God or Jesus gave when He encountered self-defeating life-styles give us pictures of the ways we can deal with such life-styles in our lives.

The response may be found through a personal encounter or a corporate encounter. We believe that God intended for human beings to live within a community, and the individual family structures and the church are the vehicles for that community. Families, therefore, become the vehicle through which the grace and love of God can be experienced.

Creative personhood is potentially possible under the grace of God. Humankind's fallen condition and continuing sinful nature has obscured the full potential of creative personhood. That personhood cannot be realized until God through Christ chooses to redeem the fallen nature. However, as the Spirit of Christ is allowed free expression in each redeemed Christian, the goal of creative personhood becomes more possible. When the Spirit of Christ empowers a redeemed community, creative personhood blossoms within each member of that community.

A natural by-product of alienation from God is the presence and domination of fear and anxiety within a person and a culture. Humans consciously experience anxiety as early as the moment of birth. As an individual grows and develops through the human life cycle, the experience of anxiety is modified. With each modification, anxiety is understood in characteristic and unique patterns within the individual. The common experience of being created, that is to say finite and alienated from an infinite and all-powerful Creator, is at the heart of human anxiety.

In 1 John 4:18-21, we find that "perfect love casts out fear." Love and fear, then, are opposed to each other mutually and neutralize the effects of each other. The experience of love neutralizing fear, or perhaps anxiety, is present in varying degrees within each individual. The degree of love depends on the individual life story of that individual. Children reared in homes which are dominated by intense anxiety, and severely limited experiences of love, do not have the internal awareness of the ways in which love can overcome the experience of anxiety. By contrast, children reared in homes with strong, emotionally secure, and spiritually mature parents have a greater internal capacity to neutralize anxiety with love. This principle seems to follow naturally from both a biblical understanding of families and a psychological understanding of human growth and development.

You will discover quickly that a creative method has been employed in uncovering the biblical stories. We offer an imaginative interpretation to familiar biblical stories. This approach is similar to the suggestions Walter Wink made in *Transforming Bible Study*. Wink compels the reader to enter the biblical text and become a part of the life situation of that text. This approach allows the reader to ask questions of the text, such as, Why or how did this event happen? or Why does the text say this and not that? or If I was in that situation, what might I have said or done? In a sense, this method allows the reader to reenact the story as if he or she were involved personally.

In our use of biblical narratives, we hope to catch a glimpse of the possible underlying themes and personalities of the characters. While every effort was made to maintain the integrity of the story, we employed our imaginations to enrich the actual biblical narrative with possible conversations and incidents that amplify the personalities of the lesser known characters of the Bible stories. This amplification, we believe, does not alter the intent of the text. Rather, we hope it enhances the flavor of each story. Perhaps you will benefit from the interpretations that this method of "personal reenactment" has offered.

Not only are biblical case studies employed in this book but psychological case studies are used as well. The best of both worlds, ancient and modern, biblical and psychological, is offered. The psychological case studies are drawn from current life situations. These contemporary case studies are representative of actual cases. No exploitation of any single person who might be known to us is intended. Indeed, the examples chosen are fictitious, and any resemblance to actual personalities is purely coincidental.

The clinical case studies are presented as simply as possible. Much of the technical psychological language has been edited out, though some remains. Ease of reading was a priority in the writing of this book. Resolutions to the self-defeating life-styles should not be misunderstood or misapplied. We caution you not to conclude that you need only to identify the similarity between a particular case study and your own life-style to resolve a serious problem. We hope that you will recognize the intricate nature of the human mind, the uniqueness of each person's life story, and the complicating interconnections of all relationships. With this in mind, the supportive care of a trained professional is stressed in each resolution of the case studies. We encourage readers who desire to be free of a self-defeating nature of their own life-styles to seek competent professional help.

Our bias is that the spiritual dimensions of these life-styles need to be addressed too. The chosen counselor, therefore, should be open to his or her own spiritual journey and allow the person seeking help to integrate the spiritual aspects of the problem with the emotional and relational aspects.

The following chapters introduce the concept of self-defeating life-styles. A life-style is a lifelong acquired pattern of behaviors and attitudes. Each life-style carries the mark of a unique strategy adopted early in life to help the individual cope with the basic human experience of anxiety.

For the purposes of this book, a clear distinction has been made between personality structure and life-style patterns of behavior and attitudes. In contemporary psychology, the concept of personality structure is used to describe the *internal* patterning of the human mind with clear characteristic defenses and predictable emotional responses to stress. We use the concept of self-defeating life-styles to refer to the more *outward* and *behavioral* evidence of a pattern of attitudes and outlook on life.

The life-styles discussed in this book are very complex. They have developed over the course of the whole life span, and each life-style contains elements in common with other life-styles. Nevertheless, they were chosen as representative examples of the dominance of a unique theme, that is, dependency, control, hostility, and so on.

Please note that certain life-styles are inclined to be attracted to each other in complementary ways. A family may have several different life-styles that interact with each other in ways that support the self-defeating qualities within each of them. Similarly, at times, the life-style pattern of one's spouse or child may confront the limitations and inadequacies of one's own style. This confrontation may encourage growth to occur naturally and spontaneously, without professional intervention or life-changing crisis. However, due to the limitations of this particular volume, we did not analyze for you these interacting patterns of different life-styles.

Here is a brief description of the twelve life-styles which are explored in this book.

Controlling: a life-style dominated by the need to be in charge or in control. The individual expects perfection from everything and shows little emotion or little mercy. The biblical illustration is Jonah.

Dependent: a life-style dominated by the inability for independent decision making. The individual must rely on others for support and stability. The biblical illustration is the resurrection appearance to Mary.

Despairing: a life-style dominated by grief, loss of hope, and loss of direction. The biblical illustration is the disciples on the road to Emmaus.

Dreamer: a life-style dominated by the inability to distinguish reality from desires or wishes. The individual shows low-level energy and application of oneself to tasks. The biblical illustration is Joseph.

Entertaining: a life-style dominated by the need for attention. The individual must have the spotlight and feels his or her only worth is to make others laugh or marvel. The biblical illustration is Simon the magician.

Handicapped: a life-style most often found in individuals

who have suffered the loss or use of physical abilities. The individual is dominated by anger, low self-esteem, and the giving of guilt to others. The biblical illustration is the healing of the lame man.

Hostile: a life-style dominated by anger, aggression, and a volatile temper. The biblical illustration is Saul.

Manipulative: a life-style dominated by conniving, underhanded, and untrusting personal interaction. The biblical illustration is Jacob.

Passive-Apathetic: a life-style dominated by others leading or controlling one's life and the unwillingness to take risks to achieve one's potential. The individual has no self worth. The biblical illustrations are the healing of the dumb man and the parable of the talents.

Power Seeking: a life-style dominated by the pursuit to get ahead, to gain money, power, or the good life. The biblical illustration is the rich young ruler.

Seductive: a life-style dominated by the need to be wanted, needed, or loved, characterized by promiscuous behavior and the treating of others as tools for an end. The biblical illustration is the woman caught in adultery.

Workaholic: a life-style dominated by the need to earn approval. The belief is that never enough is done or never done well enough. The individuals believe that the world can't survive without them. The biblical illustration is Mary and Martha.

Ask - when we play cards, what is the "trump" card?
- the card that give extra advantage.

Theme: life is not to be lived out by
manipulating **1**others to do our bidding.

The Manipulative Life-Style

Character Study: Jacob

One of the most interesting character studies in the whole Bible is the story of Jacob. Like many people, Jacob seemed to squeeze everything he could get out of life. Born the younger twin to Esau, he was by birth order denied any advantages throughout his life by Hebrew law and custom. Nevertheless, through great resourcefulness, deceit, and manipulation, Jacob managed to live life to the fullest. The story of Jacob's birth even seems descriptive of how his life and his relationships were to unfold. The picture of his emerging from his mother's womb, his hand clasped firmly upon the heel of his brother Esau, captures the essence of how he would grasp frantically at those things which others possessed. The study of Jacob's life shows us the pain, frustrations, and hollowness of his manipulative life-style, as well as the contrasting benefits that he was able to achieve.

Early in life, Jacob discovered the cunning and deceitful ways in which he could possess those things that he desired. With the assistance of his mother, who was sympathetic to his needs, he became very skilled at manipulating his environment to get what he wanted. Though we might admire his resourcefulness, his standard of right and wrong sharply

17

contrasts today's values. In Jacob's defense, however, his sense of fair play was shared by those around him in the culture of his day. The experiences of Rebekah (Gen. 27:5-17), Laban (Gen. 29:15-30; 30:31-36), and Jacob's sons (Gen. 34:13-29) are evidence that deceit was quite common and an accepted manner in relationships during Jacob's time. Even his father, Isaac, was willing to be deceitful to protect his own life and the virtue of his wife Rebekah (Gen. 26:6-11).

Jacob was so good at manipulating that his name became synonymous with that type of activity. The Hebrew word for "Jacob" or "James" might have meant "May God protect." In the development of the term, though, it came to mean "a layer of snares." You have to know Jacob's story to understand why this may be the case.

The Hebrew root word for "Jacob" refers to things which protrude, like a heel or a hill. The concept was applied to a thing which forces itself out or changes the situations or consequences. In Jacob's case, he was born grappling with his twin brother and tugging on his heel. Those who witnessed the birth and the struggle named him thus. As his life bore out, Jacob was a sly individual who crafted his own will at every opportunity. From womb to grave, Jacob schemed and connived to get his will done. He was a regular heel of a guy, always trying to find everyone else's weak points to advantage, trying to find something to trip them up. Jacob did not believe in ultimate justice or grace. He felt he had been dealt a bad hand, and it was to his advantage to change that hand.

Jacob's story begins in Genesis 25. Isaac and Rebekah were to have a child, but her pregnancy was troubled. There seemed to be a great struggle within her womb.

When the time came for her days to be accomplished, the struggle proved to be twin brothers, as different as night and day, wrestling with each other. Esau, the older, was red and hairy, destined to be a skillful hunter. Jacob, the younger, was a quiet one, a shepherd who dwelled in tents. Someone should have warned Isaac to watch out for the quiet one.

Just as Esau and Jacob fought, the struggle was reflected in the parents too. Isaac favored Esau because he loved the cooked game which Esau brought. Rebekah loved Jacob, maybe because he was the baby. Or maybe Rebekah loved Jacob because Isaac didn't. Or maybe Rebekah understood the prophecy concerning the births which stated that Esau would serve Jacob (Gen. 25:23), and she wished to be on the winning team. Whatever the case, the parental favoritism didn't help the situation.

Since Esau was the elder, all the goods and spoils were his by custom. These were exemplified as the birthright and blessing. To Jacob, this was not fair. He didn't like the way the cards were dealt, but he could correct this flaw. Once, when Esau had been out hunting and working up an appetite, Jacob slow cooked some stew. You can imagine what happened. Esau entered, hot, tired, and hungry, only to be denied Jacob's stew. After some lopsided bargaining, Jacob ended up with the birthright, Esau, only the stew. With a little wheeling and dealing, Jacob convinced Esau to sell his birthright for some red soup.

Later, in Genesis 27, when Isaac grew feeble, Jacob and his mother found a way to get the blessing also. Isaac wished to bless Esau, with all the due pomp and circumstance. Tradition required Esau to hunt some game, whip up a savory feast, and Isaac would bless him. Rebekah learned of the arrangement and plotted with Jacob to make Jacob come out ahead. Jacob and Rebekah made the meal, dressed Jacob in Esau's clothes, and wrapped goat skins around his arms to make Jacob feel like Esau. Old blind Isaac was adequately deceived and blessed Jacob with the blessing intended for Esau. During the blessing process, Jacob revealed his own theology and philosophy for life. In Genesis 27:20, Jacob stated, "Because the Lord your God granted me success." In effect, Jacob was stating his rationale that God was working in the manipulating process to grant Jacob his due. Jacob layed a snare and caught both Esau and Isaac. Now he believed he had corrected the flaw of life, his misdealt hand.

Mortals were not the only ones who dealt with Jacob's trickery. In Genesis 28:13-22, Jacob encountered God at Bethel, where God openly stated, "I will be your God, I will bring you back to this land, it will all work out" (author's paraphrase). That wasn't enough for Jacob. He made an altar and a new deal, "If God does what He says He will do, gives me food and clothing, and I can come home in peace, then I will worship Him and give Him the tithe" (author's paraphrase). Jacob even failed to find justice and grace with God.

Not all of Jacob's deals worked to his advantage. Jacob made a deal with Laban for his younger daughter, Rachel, in Genesis 29:15-20. Laban got even for everybody, though, because Jacob ended up with Leah, the older daughter, instead of Rachel. Now Rachel was beautiful to behold, but Leah had weak eyes. Jacob was very disappointed when he discovered Laban's deception. Eventually, Jacob had to double his bargain to get Rachel. What goes around comes around. So Jacob got manipulated now and then also.

Rachel experienced the greatest injustice, however. She was barren. In those days, that was like having no gender or no useful purpose. By Genesis 30, Leah and the two maids had given birth to numerous sons, but Rachel continued to be barren. Finally, after much painful waiting, Rachel bore two sons, who turned out to be Jacob's favorites.

Laban evidently was quite the manipulator too. He not only dealt in daughters but herds as well (Gen. 30:31 ff.). When Jacob and Laban bargained for the sheep and goats, they agreed that Jacob would get anything that was blemished (v. 32). Jacob thought he had won because the majority of the herds had some stripe or mark on them. Laban solved that little discrepancy by sending all the marked animals three days' journey away. Not to be outdone, Jacob worked out a breeding procedure whereby the remaining sheep produced speckled offspring. Jacob ended up with the younger, stronger portion of the herd.

Jacob and Esau were destined to meet again, and Jacob wasn't looking forward to the meeting. In Genesis 32, Jacob felt that Esau was still very angry with him, so he sent all of his women, herds, and children to meet Esau. Perhaps he hoped Esau might feel sorry for him if he saw all of Jacob's family and financial obligations. Jacob tried to disarm Esau even in reconciliation.

Later Jacob wrestled with an angel all night. In Genesis 32:25, the Bible says when the angel saw that he could "not prevail against Jacob, he touched the hollow of his thigh," and put it "out of joint." Even the messengers of the most high God could not wrestle a square deal with Jacob. In fact, Jacob did not release the angel until he had wrestled a blessing out of him.

In Genesis 34, Jacob's daughter, Dinah, was raped. The

offender asked to marry Dinah. Jacob's sons' anger was not so easily dissipated. They made the offender and his male kin be circumcised before she could marry. While they were recovering from that ordeal, Simeon and Levi killed them.

There never seemed enough justice or grace for Jacob. He just pushed and shoved and pushed and shoved until everything was messed up. All Jacob could ever understand was that somehow God was bringing him success if he manipulated. But to deny the justice and grace of God, even face-to-face, is inappropriate. When Jacob woke up and felt like he had been mistreated through the actions of his sons, he should have remembered his words of the morning at Bethel (Gen. 28:16), "Surely the Lord is in this place; and I did not know it." Even in the worst of circumstances, God is present, open to offer assistance, but not necessarily easy solutions.

To Jacob's credit, we recognize his resourcefulness and persistence at overcoming great personal and cultural limitations. Desiring opportunities equal to those of his older brother (and older by only a few minutes at that!), Jacob found ways to neutralize Esau's unfair advantage and become his brother's equal. He chose not to let the culturally determined values of birth order and success limit his own future opportunities. He discovered that both his father and brother responded instantaneously to their intense need for physical pleasure and comfort. With little critical reflection, they would impulsively surrender cherished beliefs and values when tempted to receive immediate gratification for the needs of pleasure and comfort. Jacob realized that people see what they want to see to justify their getting the short-term gratification that they desire. In this sense, Jacob realized that his brother and his father were very much like

him. We might admire this insightfulness into human behavior and motivation and applaud Jacob's initiative, but
we dislike the extent to which he went in his deceit to win
the prize.

The Jacob story of trickery and deceit has a very familiar
ring. Even today with our post-Mosaic rules for living and
our less constricting social and cultural values, we are familiar with Jacob's life-style. One need not wrestle with angels
to feel the need to manipulate the environment.

Case Study: Gary

Gary sought a pastoral counselor because he felt that
every significant person in his life was angry with him. Being the manager of a local discount department store, Gary
suspected that not only his employees but also his wife and
three children were against him. His employees, with
whom he had always thought he had a warm and friendly
relationship, were beginning to pull away from him and be
involved in activities that he felt were disloyal to both him
and the company. Everything he tried to do to please Sue,
his wife, seemed to backfire into episodes of intense conflict
and disharmony. His kids never wanted to participate in the
events he planned for them to share together. Gary felt angry, dissatisfied, and depressed. His moods fluctuated from
one to the next to the next. He asked the counselor what
could be done to get everyone to be more cooperative with
him again.

As the counseling relationship unfolded, Gary's pastoral
counselor discovered that this was the first time in Gary's
memory that he had not been able to get his way or to per-
suade people to see his point of view. Growing up in the
same church where he was still an active member, and be-

ing one of the minister's children, Gary fondly told stories from his youth in which he constantly enjoyed the affirmation and attention he got as a result of being the minister's son. He quietly confessed to having discovered how to "read people" early in life as a way of discerning how to respond to them in order to have them meet his needs. He quickly discovered that being cute, witty, and willing to stretch the truth just a little bit would frequently and consistently produce the responses he wanted from others. Using this strategy, he got what he wanted and thought he needed.

Gary always managed to get good enough grades to be elected into significant leadership positions of groups at school and church. He was the constant recipient of the generosity of other people in the form of gifts of money, rides home from various functions, and other special "favors." He even managed to get his first job at the department store as a high school student by having his father call the manager of the store. Using some ministerial persuasion on a church member, his dad arranged for Gary to be employed in the stockroom when he was technically still underage. Gary worked at the store off and on through high school a couple of evenings a week and Saturdays and during the summer. He gradually climbed up the ladder. He gained more and more responsibilities until he became the first manager appointed to that position at the age of twenty-six! Gary's telling of this story reflected a sense of pride with an accompanying underlying expression of self-doubt and anxiety.

As the counseling continued, further illustrations of Gary's unique ability to use people to get what he wanted began to unfold. Gary tried to get the counselor to make a special appointment for him in the early evening after work, even in the face of the counselor's insistence that he never saw people after five o'clock. Gary protested that the counselor really didn't care for people but was only interested in collecting a fee. Gary threatened not to pay his fee because he wasn't getting what he wanted in the counseling process. The pastoral counselor himself experienced feelings of anger and distrust and began to wonder what motives Gary might have behind every question or request that was raised. The counseling finally terminated prematurely after the counselor confronted Gary for missing an appointment with no advanced warning and for refusing to make any payments on the bill that had been accumulating. His counselor called to ask for an explanation. He shared his concern that Gary might not understand the inconvenience that he was creating by his irresponsibility. Gary exploded in anger on the phone and ended the pastoral counseling relationship.

Analysis of the Manipulative Life-Style

Gary might be understood as a modern-day Jacob. Gary's early sense of right and wrong was influenced by the special attention he received as a minister's son. Like Jacob responding to Rebekah's overattentiveness, Gary learned at an early age how to get what he wanted from the significant "others" in his world by playing to their need to smother him with unearned favors. Rebekah needed to have a special relationship with Jacob that was different in quality and degree in how she related to Esau. Gary was able to sense when the parishioners in the church were willing to find special favor in his father's eyes by giving the minister's son special attention and unearned favors.

Gary learned how to "play to the audience's needs" and to say and do what he perceived people wanted to see and hear. Minor modifications and embellishments of the truth were greeted with smiles, nods, and other signs that people were pleased with his creative wit and imagination. Gradually Gary lost control over his temptations to distort the truth and manipulate people through giving them false performances instead of open honesty. He became quite successful, and his behavior became automatic as he learned to insulate himself from his conscience and to rationalize away his actions. Finally, Gary was unable to tolerate the intense anxiety of truth and reality. His "game" became hollow enough that other people realized what was really happening. His significant relationships at home, work, and church became increasingly complicated and out of control. Gary's primary strategy for coping with life had become a bigger problem than the anxieties with which he was trying to cope.

Gary had learned to expect from everyone that his decisions would be accepted without challenge. He was devastated by the suspiciousness with which others constantly responded to his initiatives. The pain of his past and continuing deceptions could not be denied or rationalized away any longer.

In all fairness to Gary, it is understandable and applaudable that as a little boy, overwhelmed and overstimulated by the demands of the adults in his life, he learned how to please others as a coping response to anxieties. The choice of the path of least resistance is quite resourceful. Gary's path was to respond to these pressures through strategies designed to please others instead of frustrating others. In the choice of this path, however, Gary developed a "false self" characterized by manipulation. Gary's false self eventually covered over and dominated the "true self" which was too frightened to show itself. Gradually Gary was unable to distinguish the "false" from the "true." He identified solely with the manipulating life-style as the real and only Gary. His identification was so complete that he was genuinely offended when others, including the pastoral counselor, attributed distasteful qualities and motives to his behavior.

A Word of Hope

Gary will have great difficulty overcoming his manipulating life-style. It is so much a part of him that he will not be able to distinguish which behavioral responses are related to the problem. Like Jacob, Gary misunderstands human needs and God's grace. The core of Gary's self-defeating life-style problem is the mistaken belief that he cannot be open or honest to his advantage. He believes that he must deceive, trick, or control every situation to gain an advantage. He ignores whatever his gifts or strengths might be, whatever the situation or relationship might offer, or whatever someone else might need in favor of how he can use the moment to get ahead.

Jacob didn't believe in the grace of God. His every action was an attempt to correct what he perceived was an unjust situation. If Jacob didn't correct it, no one would. Gary's actions do not stem from a sense of injustice but from the need to have an advantage. Both individuals, though, used the same method to attain their respective ends. Both individuals needed to come to grips with the reality of the human predicament which includes some injustice and some disadvantage.

If we could compare life to a game of cards, good advice for life would be to play the hand that you are dealt. Don't worry about what might have been or whether someone has something you can't have. Don't even worry whether you have the best hand at all. Simply make the best of what you have, play the hand you are dealt, and go on. From this perspective, life's real challenge is not to correct injustice or make the other players like you. Rather, life's challenge is to play the best hand possible, even without holding any trump cards. Now on the other side of the issue, all of us know folk who are never satisfied with what they have. They always want a redeal in the card game of life. They don't believe in either justice or grace, or they just want more. Invariably, these Garys or Jacobs contrive every situation to get the most possible personal advantage.

Jesus Christ has affirmed the human condition. We do not need to manipulate others' affections or possessions if Christ has truly regarded our humble estate. If Christ can accept us as we are, we must be worth something. Gary will have to relearn to accept himself, as Christ has accepted him. Only through receiving God's love for us in Christ can we be satisfied with ourselves. Only then can we agree with the words of the hymnist, "It is well with my soul."

2

The Passive-Apathetic Life-Style

Case Study: Allen

Allen works part-time as a stock boy in a grocery store. He is thirty-five years old, single and still lives in his parent's home. Allen has worked at this same grocery store for eighteen years, since he started earning money for his first car. Allen had been a bright student, though for years his teachers lamented his lack of motivation in applying himself to reach his academic potential.

Allen has an older sister who captured the spotlight since childhood. She was a child prodigy, a gifted musician, even before grade school. She succeeded in finishing both high school and college at an accelerated pace—gifted and talented the whole way. At family gatherings, Allen would sit quietly while the various members of the clan stood amazed in the presence of his sister. She could play any of their favorite songs by ear. Occasionally Allen would offer a suggestion of a tune, or a waltz for his sister's benefit, and then retreat into the adoring audience.

Allen survived in school because of a better-than-average intelligence. He never enjoyed any sense of personal achievement, so he never seemed to catch the teacher's attention. Often he would have to listen to a teacher's retelling of the marvelous escapades of his older sister. Of course, this usually only happened whenever he had the misfortune of following her with the same teacher. After a while, Allen got used to this process year in and year out. He gave up worrying about trying to impress them with his own uniqueness or showing them that he was different from his sister. His parents quit trying to motivate him as well and seemed satisfied if his grades were acceptable or he didn't need any obvious help or attention.

As Allen matured, he showed little interest in sports, dating girls, or other interests of boys his age. His passion was restoring the 1956 Chevy that he had purchased with the money from his job as stock boy at the store. After graduation from high school, Allen debated about entering the military service and learning a skill, but he decided not to out of fear that he would not be trained in the specialty of his choice. Instead, he attended the local community college for a few semesters. When it came time to declare a major and begin to take advanced courses, Allen was uninspired by any of his choices. So he dropped out of college.

Allen's parents are worried about his lack of successfulness and his willingness to stay at home. They would prefer that he find a career with a future and move out on his own. His mother is somewhat protective and feels partly responsible for Allen's lack of motivation. She recognizes that she was overly involved with her daughter's successes. Consequently, she is unable to confront Allen aggressively, put him out of the house, or insist that he grow up to accept more responsibility for his life. Every conversation she has with Allen ends the same way. He shrugs his shoulders, indicates that he doesn't see what her objections are all about, and reminds her that she has one more successful child than most parents are privileged to have.

When a new choir director was hired at church, Allen's listlessness changed. This young and attractive woman learned of Allen's family's musical history and asked Allen to join the choir. Upon hearing his pleasant voice, she offered him a solo in the Christmas cantata.

Now Allen faces a real predicament. He is caught between his desire to impress this woman who seems genuinely interested in *his* talent and potential and his own anxiety about performing for the first time in his life. Nervously, he confesses his anxiety to the choir director, who offers to give him private voice lessons in preparation for the cantata. Her continuing attention and praise encourages Allen's affections, and a new problem emerges. Allen realizes that he is in love for the first time with a very successful woman, with no experience or personal successes to fall back on. He gradually becomes acutely depressed, and barely survives the ordeal of the Christmas performance. Following the performance, Allen is distraught and begins to withdraw again in reaction to his lack of structured opportunities to be with the object of his affections. In desperation, he calls the associate pastor and shares his sense of hopelessness.

Allen is trapped in a passive life-style. He is used to being unnoticed, and he can't find a way to be rescued. One wonders how many like Allen go unnoticed in the world. In our own hectic schedules, who are the individuals that we overlook each day?

Character Study: The Speechless One

The Bible offers us a story about an unnoticed person. In Luke 11:14 and following, we read, "Now he was casting out a demon that was dumb; when the demon had gone out, the dumb man spoke, and the people marveled. But some of them said, 'He casts out demons by Beelzebul, the prince of demons.'"

We don't know this man's name, perhaps he didn't have one. At least, no one ever heard him say it. All we know is these few lines from the Gospel of Luke. So we don't have much of a biography to draw from in understanding the full nature of the man's problem.

Who can say what prohibits one from speaking? Is it only a unusual abnormality in the brain that hinders the speech function? Does one have to be born with a defect or have an injury to the brain to lose the ability to talk? Many of us would admit that there are a number of circumstances that might keep us from speaking. Silence might be chosen in circumstances of fear or of either physical or emotional harm. There are also moments where, for whatever the reason, the timing was not right to speak: someone else had the floor, your mouth was full of food, special delivery arrived, etc. We can all identify with a time when we really should have spoken and didn't. Now imagine having been raised in an environment where you never had an opportunity to speak. How about being told daily that you can't and then not being given the chance to try? A physical defect might cause you to be speechless, but a suppressive environment also can reduce one to a quiet, passive individual.

So in this particular story, a man is reported to be afflicted by demons and unable to speak. Perhaps he sulked around on the back row of life, with no friends and never looking individuals in the eye. He may have shown no concern about his appearance because no one cared about him, and perhaps he was always scaring others with his silence and rude stares. He just wandered around, hearing bits and pieces of information ranging from idle talk to serious plans. Folk said what they pleased around him because no one believed that he was smart enough for it to matter. People pushed him from side to side because they didn't care. He didn't seem to care either. He was just in the way when he was seen. He just didn't exist when he was not seen.

Jesus changed all of that. Instead of making fun of the dumb man, ignoring him, or pushing him out of the way, Jesus took him seriously and healed him. The formerly speechless man spoke, and a mixed reaction was drawn from the crowd. The Scripture says that the people marveled, which was a common response to the miracles of Jesus. Other people accused Jesus of dealing in the demonic. On the whole, that is how people react to change: Some marvel and are awestruck, while others make accusations.

Nothing more is known of the dumb man. He had been given a new outlook on life, and perhaps a brand-new life. Where do you suppose he went? Do you think he returned to his old ways of not talking? I doubt it. Do you think he was spiteful and sought revenge on any or all who abused him? Perhaps, but I imagine some other things took place which outweighed revenge. I think he went and said some special words to his favorite people. I imagine he went and told a joke or listened for his echo or screamed as loud as he could. I think for years to come he never missed the opportunity to say the right think to someone who needed to hear it. He had spent too many years witnessing the hurt of ill-chosen words and the bondage of noncorrective silence.

Biblical Illustration of Passivity

The concept of passivity and apathy are not specifically

referred to in the Bible. Slothfulness, though, is repeatedly mentioned, and with a harsh tone of judgment. A familiar character who displayed an almost apathetic life-style is the slothful servant in the parable of the talents of Matthew 25:14-30. Listen with new ears to a retelling of that parable.

The master was going on a journey and needed someone to look after his property. Being an open-minded sort of man, he decided to leave his property under the watchful care of three servants. Now the master knew the servants' personalities and abilities, and he gave to each of them accordingly. To the first servant, he gave five hundred gold pieces, to the second, two hundred gold pieces, and to the third, one hundred gold pieces.

The servant with five hundred gold pieces was an industrious man. After the master had left, he wanted to increase his master's money, even though five hundred gold pieces was more money than he ever hoped to see. In fact, ten gold pieces was more than an average man might ever earn. This was fifty times that amount. What does one do with so great an amount of wealth? He went out and consulted with those who knew how to make money and invested the whole amount. That was quite a gamble considering the amount of money and whose money it was. You remember, the master didn't say, "Go, invest my money." But the servant wanted to make good on the master's trust. By a stroke of luck, the first servant doubled his investment.

The second servant followed the example of the first, and invested his master's two hundred gold pieces. Sure enough, this servant doubled his original investment as well. Now the third servant didn't care much for responsibility. It wasn't his money; he wasn't going to get anything from it, so he just put the one hundred gold pieces aside. He refused to take the risks the other servants took.

When the master returned, he inquired about his property. The first servant proudly presented the master with one thousand gold pieces. The master was very surprised. "Where did this extra money come from?" he asked. The first servant told how he had invested the money and doubled its value. The master was surprised at the first servant. "You're pretty brave with someone else's money, aren't you? Well done! Here, keep the original five hundred gold pieces."

When the second servant presented his amount, the master was equally surprised. "What manner of madness led you to risk my wealth? What if you had lost it all? Well, such is the gamble of life. You did well. Here, keep the original investment."

As the third servant arrived, the master could not contain himself. "Friend, tell me, what has become of the one hundred gold pieces I gave you?" The third servant replied, "Well, since it was your money, I let it sit around until you got back." The master could only reply, "Why? Didn't you see what the others did? Didn't you care?" The servant answered, "It wasn't mine. You asked me to watch it, and I did." The master then said to the others, "Take the one hundred gold pieces from him and send him away from our house. He is not a part of us. He could not take risks and could not see the benefit in another's gain. He looks only after himself."

A Word of Hope

Healing in the New Testament is a picture of salvation. When one was healed physically, we witness an image of spiritual salvation. Usually the healed one praised God, went and told others, and brought them to Jesus. The picture changes from the unhealed passive individual to the healed independent and assertive individual. Salvation brings total wholeness: acceptance of physical limitations, cleansing of emotional drawbacks, and new directions in spiritual awakenings.

Allen had chosen a self-imposed silence to avoid the anxiety of comparisons with his more gifted and talented older sister. Rather than risk comparison and being considered inadequate against her exceptional standard, Allen avoided comparison with any standard, including his own. The issue of risk is at the heart of his choice to seek passivity as a life-style. His strategy was useful to avoid embarrassment and the experience of being discounted when living in the shadow of his sister. The strategy became self-defeating when Allen chose to respond to all situations with passivity rather than to risk the anxiety of competition. His low self-worth in his family became the rationale for avoiding opportunities to establish his worthiness in other settings.

Allen was guilty of the sin of failing to be a person in his own right. His low self-esteem was greater than his comparison to his unusual sister and became the by-product of his unwillingness to risk a commitment to any course requiring a test of his abilities. He avoided a career in the military, a commitment to a college major, and the multiple commitments that come in any dating relationships. Sadly, it took the interest of an exceptional young woman, the minister of music at his church, to spark his investment in becoming a person of worth. At this point in his life, the stakes were so high that risking success precipitated an intense depression. The prize of winning this young woman's affections overwhelmed him because he had no experience at risking and succeeding to fall back on. And yet something of a spark of self-affirmation had been ignited within him as a result of her sincere interest in him as a person. He could no longer hide within the safety of his passive-apathetic life-style and conveniently blame his sister, his parents, or anyone else for his lack of personal fulfillment. The truth was known to Allen at last. It was his choice to avoid the anxiety of taking a risk that produced the self-defeating quality of his life.

In a manner of speaking, Allen's encounter with this minister of music was similar to the encounter of the dumb man with Jesus. The dumb man was affirmed by Jesus as a person of worth in spite of his limitations. His healing was not only physical but also restored him to a spiritual state of self-acceptance and inspired him to live his life to its fullest potential. In the eyes of this attractive female musician, Allen had worth greater than he had ever experienced. The self-defeating dimension of his passive life-style was exposed, and the spiritual consequences of his failure to take risks was also revealed to him.

Likewise, Allen's experience is very similar to the parable of the three servants. Like the third servant, Allen chose not to develop his talents but to bury them in the ground. Years of investment potential were unrealized. Instead of drawing interest on his potential, Allen was content to let his skills and abilities lie dormant and undeveloped.

We have all been dumb. We do not know how to say what we most want to say, be it to ourselves, each other, or God. We also struggle with the temptation to avoid the risks of life and to discover the full potential of our abilities, like the third servant in Jesus's parable. Jesus understands our dilemma and frees us to speak. Empowered by the joy and acceptance of His love, we become willing to change our perspective, alter our life-styles of passivity and apathy, and accept the challenges and risks of living.

3

The Dependent Life-Style

My two-year-old loves his mother. He adores her. He holds on to her hand, he tugs at her leg, and he whines to get her attention. He is afraid to be out of her sight. I guess he thinks the worst might happen if she isn't there to stabilize his life. Yes, James is completely dependent on his mother. There is nothing wrong with that relationship. Most children should feel dependent on their parents. As the child develops, though, the tendency to be dependent on the parent should diminish. For some, the parental dependency is replaced with personal independence. For others, parental dependency is replaced with another dependent relationship.

Case Study: Sara

Sara is a widowed mother of two children, Karen (age twenty) and Ronnie (age fifteen). Four years have passed since Bob's death. Sara works full-time as a legal secretary. This income, in combination with her husband's very adequate insurance policies, provides a comfortable living. Sara and Bob's stormy marriage had lasted seventeen years and included one brief separation after Ronnie's birth. The months just preceding Bob's death, however, seemed like a second honeymoon. Bob had received a significant promotion and had given up his pattern of heavy drinking, after years of trying to control his drinking patterns unsuccessfully.

Sara sought her pastor's help because she didn't feel she had her life on track. She knew that most of her mourning was past because she wasn't overwhelmed with feelings of grief and loss as she had been during that first year after Bob's death. However, Sara didn't feel that she was a whole person, and she was overly preoccupied with finding a new spouse. Several of her friends and family had commented to her that she seemed too "desperate and lonely" for her own good.

The children, too, were affected. Sara refused to allow them the freedom to pursue the normal interests of teenagers. A big conflict had emerged between her and Karen last summer. Karen intended to move out of her bedroom at home and live in the college dormitory. Karen's reasons stemmed from the smothering way that Sara treated her in refusing to let Karen grow up. Ronnie, too, was pulling away from Sara. Ever since he hit puberty, Ronnie seemed to be getting into more trouble at school. A school counselor suggested to Sara that Ronnie's behavior problems might be a message to her that he had a mind and will of his own.

These confrontations with her family and friends had devastated Sara. She was no longer able to determine whether she was loving her children too much or using them to fill the emotional vacuum in her life left by Bob's death. After a few sessions of weekly counseling with her pastor, he suspected that she was becoming more dependent upon him than was emotionally or spiritually wise. Sara found excuses to call him on the phone between her counseling sessions for advice, and she frequently stopped him in the hallway of the church in order to get a few minutes of his attention between services and meetings at the church.

Sara's pastor knew that many of her requests for advice and support were about issues she was capable of resolving on her own. She began to report to him in their counseling sessions that no one cared for her as he did. She preferred to wait and hear his counsel before responding to any suggestions from other friends or even following her own initiative and responses. Sara was having dreams that were very disturbing to her because of their clear implication of a growing sexual attraction to her pastor who was much younger than she was. After several weeks of extreme anxiety as a result of these dreams, she confessed their content to her pastor and anticipated his scolding her for her indecent thoughts and intentions. To her great surprise, her pastor seemed to be concerned, but not threatened, by her confessions.

The pastor sought to steer Sara toward separating her dependency from him and discovering her own identity apart from the counseling relationship. Sara became aware that she had replaced Bob, Karen, and Ronnie with her pastor. She realized a pattern that she had developed from childhood of overinvesting in one significant relationship to the exclusion of the development of intimate relationships with a variety of individuals. The dependent relationship moved from her mother, to Bob, to her kids, and now to her pastor. Sara was unable to describe any uniqueness in her own personal identity outside of the roles she had in these relationships.

Conflict Between Dependence and Independence

How does one move from dependency to independency?

An initial step is to recognize the presence of the dependent life-style. A second step is to recognize the inherent fear in that life-style. The dependent person is afraid of being independent, of being responsible for one's own decisions. The fear can be expressed in terms of failure or of encountering too great an obstacle.

Each of us in our maturing process invests life in a series of significant relationships with family, friends, co-workers, and the like. Our lives become blended with others' lives in a healthy exchange of opinions and strengths. Our fears are covered and supported in the strengths and experiences of others. When an individual begins to lose his or her decision-making ability to others, that individual is moving in the direction of a dependent life-style.

One might question whether Sara was doing anything wrong. After all, she was seeking help from her pastor. Yes, if she only were seeking help, Sara was making a good choice. Sara's problem, though, was allowing her pastor to govern her every move. Religious leaders are not exempt from followers granting them too much control. Today's headlines are full of folk who have allowed religious leaders to control their lives. Even Jesus encountered this problem.

Character Study: Mary

Remember the appearance of Jesus to Mary Magdalene in John 20? Peter and John had raced to the grave on Easter morning. The two had gone when they saw His tomb was empty. Mary could not believe it. She had felt that she would die too when Jesus was killed. She loved Him so much, she needed Him to live. After the faithful had buried Jesus, Mary had convinced herself to go on living. The only saving factor had been that at least she knew where Jesus was buried. When she needed some consolation or needed to be near His body, Mary at least could visit Jesus' grave. Now the body was gone too. Someone not only had removed His touch, His words, and His life but also had removed the only remembrance she had—His body. Mary feared that she had been left with nothing of Jesus to cling to, and her tears flowed quickly.

Mary turned to find a stranger watching her. "Miss, why are you crying? Tell me who it is that you miss," He asked. "If you took Him," began Mary, "tell me where He is. I must know where His body is, so that I can have it." The stranger answered, "Mary, tell me who it is that you miss." "Jesus," Mary whispered. "Oh, Jesus," she said, and she rushed to hold Him.

Jesus did a surprising thing. He wouldn't let Mary touch Him. She wailed, "Master, please hold me. I need you." Jesus replied, "No, Mary. Don't cling to me, for I must first ascend to my Father. Go and tell the disciples what you have witnessed here." It is very surprising to us that Jesus would not allow Mary to embrace Him. The reasons He wouldn't allow her to touch Him are unknown to us and will remain a mystery for now. Suppose, however, that Jesus was trying to respond to Mary's unusual dependence upon Him and was suggesting an alternative that she had to consider if she were going to continue to grow as a person and in the faith. Let's paraphrase this conversation, reflecting this insight as it may have been.

Jesus replied, "No, Mary. You have misunderstood me. I can't let you cling to me anymore. You weren't supposed to give up being yourself and attach yourself to Me in this way. I hoped that you would find your life with Me, but you have lost it. Instead of becoming a responsible person, you've become completely dependent on Me. You've lost the ability to choose for yourself because you have relinquished both your desires and fears to Me. Out of misguided devotion, you are refusing to decide your own life. I can't carry you like this. You should go on with life as I have."

"But Jesus," Mary urged, "I can't go on. I need You." Jesus said, "No, Mary. You don't need Me to be physically present with you. You have a new life. You are responsible and free to choose what that life will be. By God's grace, you are free even to make mistakes because you know that God can forgive you. Now go and tell the disciples what you know. The disciples have My blessing to carry on this ministry. They will become the carriers of My truth and will help the church begin to live and grow in My absence. They can help you face the future without Me to lean on. They will encourage you to become everything God created you to be!"

Analysis of Dependent Life-Style

Both Sara and Mary had allowed their lives to become so intertwined with another, that they were in danger of losing their own individuality and separate identities. The desire to maintain an infantile state of complete dependency upon another person is a common fantasy and is at the core of the dependent life-style. Deep within each individual is the memory of the experience of infancy, in which every need was responded to by the mothering person. Mother seemed to be an extension of our own personhood. If we were hungry, food was provided. If we had soiled our diapers, the clean diaper was provided. If we were cold, a warm covering appeared. Every discomfort that was encountered was responded to immediately by this "all-knowing" alter ego of our selves. Full responsibility for our comforts and necessities of life was taken by this extension of our fragile and very self-absorbed egos.

Many individuals continue in this fantasy long after the reality of a world with frustration has replaced the illusion of the self-absorbed infant. Some parents foster this dependent fantasy in an effort to provide loving support for each other while at the same time denying the children their much-needed opportunities to solve life's problems by themselves. Parents also enjoy the power and significance that they experience when their children continue to need them long after it is appropriate. Many parents feel so inadequate and worthless that a dependent child gives them a sense of meaning and purpose that would otherwise be absent. The void of one's own identity becomes filled with the presence of another.

The natural human life cycle requires a state of dependency during infancy and early childhood. However, with increasing age and personal competency to solve one's own problems, the healthy individual emerges from childhood desiring more independence and separateness from the parents during adolescence and young adulthood. The continuing need to be related to another is satisfied in the teenage years with the rise of importance of the peer group. The peer group takes over many of the functions of dependent relating that the parents had provided in the early years. After an appropriate time of separation from the identity of parents and family, the young adult usually emerges capable of establishing a significant relationship of interdependence with someone of the opposite sex. Marriage is the desired way of structuring this state of interdependence.

Adults who have been reared in homes in which dependency upon the parents is expected and fostered are attracted frequently to mates who will allow them to continue to live "through" another individual. Usually, though not necessarily always, this is the situation for women. Due to the history of male dominance in Western culture, women are inclined to seek strong males who will take care of them like their parents did. Afraid to make decisions on their own and needing someone else to take care of them, these women seek a mate who can fulfill these basic dependent needs. Like Sara, they become so emotionally attached to their husbands and children that, in the event of the early tragic death of their spouse or the inevitable growing away of their children, they are left with no sense of their personhood alone.

Our society encourages this tragic condition in many subtle ways. We frequently rear our daughters with a different set of expectations than our sons. Girls are conditioned to see themselves as "growing up, getting married, having children, and rearing a family" as the only worthwhile goals for their lives. In spite of the women's liberation movement of the last twenty years, many young women still feel guilty if they choose a single life-style with a professional focus instead of marriage and children. If they try to attempt both career and family, the wife/mother ends up feeling full responsibility for being the primary caretaker of husband and children and professional peers.

A Word of Hope

Many marriages occur between two individuals who want to perpetuate the romantic myth of: "You and me, against the world." This myth is built on the assumption that two lives merged completely can by themselves withstand any challenge that life offers. The well-known biblical prescription for marriage of 1 Corinthians 6:16 is that "two shall become one." However, this scriptural admonition does not mean necessarily what our popular cultural interpretation has assumed. Many couples falsely assume that this text is the description of the fused identity of two dependent personalities who find a sense of identity only in the marriage relationship. Their fear is that they have no separate identities to fall back on.

Our belief is that the marriage union provides a new identity for each separate individual, that includes both a sense of "we" as well as a continuing awareness of "you" and "me." This belief is based on the necessity of two fully developed "selves" who can choose to become related in a shared union of equals. This union is not a merger of one inferior self with a more superior self, or a merger of two inferior selves into a single superior self (we).

The dependent life-style emerges with a variety of external influences which encourage the internal need to relate to a significant other individual. As we have discussed, the need to be in relationship is natural from birth onward but can become distorted in those individuals who never discover how to be alone or maintain a sense of their own identity. As in the case of Sara, the dependent individual needs opportunities and encouragement to become self-sufficient. Interests and abilities can be encouraged outside of the primary relationships of one's life without necessarily competing with these relationships.

The church becomes a place where one's identity as a separate child of God is affirmed, and healthy opportunities to be related in a state of mutual interdependency is encouraged. The understanding of the church as the "family of God" with each individual member playing an important role in the total function of the family is held in tension with the 1 Corinthians 12 model of the church as "the body of Christ." The individual "members" of the "body" are interconnected with each other, so the whole body can perform the necessary functions of life. Perhaps it was this model of the functioning church that Christ was pointing to in His instructions to Mary to seek out the disciples and become part of that fellowship. Mary could overcome this life-style and find her independence in the interdependence of the body of believers.

4

The Hostile Life-Style

Character Study: Saul

There wasn't a better choice for Israel's king than Saul. First Samuel 9:2 offers this description and account of Saul. He had all the right qualities, including wealth, good looks, and leadership ability. In fact, the Bible records that he was head and shoulders above the competition. When it came time for the Jews to have a king, God chose Saul. Think of that, chosen and anointed of God to be king. Who could ask for anything more?

Saul was not only the people's choice but also God's choice to be ruler. The conversation about him in those days was "the spirit of the Lord" was mighty upon him. Saul was mighty, particularly in battle. No enemy could withstand Saul's armies while the Spirit of the Lord was with him. Maybe this was where the trouble started. Maybe Saul lost touch with the humanity of the office and began to view himself only as the warrior leader. He began to take matters into his own hands. The battles became more bloody and more frequent. The divine purposes for the battles were lost in the hostile and violent ways Saul went about achieving victory. On occasion, Saul disobeyed God intentionally, and God became dissatisfied with Saul. The Spirit of the Lord was withdrawn from Saul and was replaced with an evil spirit more akin to the hostile life-style Saul had chosen.

We know from our Bible study that eventually Saul and David met each other. David was God's new choice to be king. Saul was not happy with that idea, but he was enamored with David. You see, when Saul lost his temper and broke out with violent rage, David came and played the lyre to soothe Saul. The Bible doesn't explain why the music of the lyre had this effect on Saul, but perhaps Saul's response was similar to our own. Music can relax us, release anxiety, calm the storms of fears that face us, or place us in touch with our deepest emotions. Music can cause us to stop, to change course mid thought, to laugh, or to cry. My friend Darrell Adams has that effect on me. When he sings and plays the guitar, a flood of memories and emotions encompass me, leaving me at his mercy. Such was David's effect on Saul.

The relationship between David and Saul was fragile, however. Increasingly, Saul became anxious about David's growing popularity. It was only a matter of time before Saul's rage was directed toward David. The people began to laud David as a better warrior than Saul. Saul could not live with that. Whether Saul possessed the Spirit of the Lord or an evil spirit, Saul's identity was wrapped up in being the finest warrior in Israel.

Saul banished David from his home and sought ways to defeat him in battle. However, his planned confrontation with David on the battlefield never took place. At the moment the war was lost, when it was apparent that Saul would lose his kingship and his great warrior status, Saul chose to turn his hostility upon himself. He fell on his own sword, killing himself.

What a tragic misreading of the options in Saul's life. David, whom Saul believed to be his greatest rival, also offered the release he really sought. The hostile life-style is frequently characterized by conflicting feelings about the important people in our lives. Those who offer us our greatest aid and support are the very ones upon whom our hostility is released.

Case Study: Carl

Carl was a twenty-year-old college junior when he dropped by to see his pastor one Saturday afternoon. He said that he was sad and preoccupied. He couldn't concentrate on his studies since his girl friend, Sharon, had broken up with him three weeks earlier. He wasn't sure, but he believed Sharon ended their engagement because he had little control over his temper. "I can't help it," he said, "she just makes me so angry, I lose control." Carl then described a pattern of emotional abuse, combined with occasional physical outbursts, that even frightened himself.

Carl came from a family in which explosive outbursts were common. His father, who supported the family of six by driving a truck cross-country, came home on weekends, usually after he stopped off at a tavern on the way. As was the pattern, Carl's mother met his daddy at the door and unloaded her frustration from a week of parenting four little boys by herself. Tired and intoxicated, his father then would explode in violent rage that often lasted throughout the weekend. Come Monday morning, Carl's father left for the next out-of-town trip.

Though not physically abusive, Carl's mother also frequently got angry and expressed her anxiety and disappointment with verbal assaults on her children. Carl remembered those assaults as being more painful than any his dad gave him on the weekend.

Carl admitted to overdrinking, which he knew disappointed Sharon. He also confessed that he was jealous and overly possessive of Sharon. Since Sharon was a very attractive, popular coed at the college they attended, Carl's jealousy was a constant problem. Carl was argumentative with his teachers in the classroom and frequently lost his temper during varsity basketball games. He embarrassed himself and the entire team with the tantrums that he would throw frequently. "No matter how hard I try," Carl said, "I just can't seem to control this fire inside of me!" The friends who had still stuck with him all tried to show Carl alternative ways of dealing with his frustrations, but no one else's system seemed to work for him.

In desperation, Carl turned to his pastor for help. Something that was said in the previous Sunday's sermon about anger caught Carl's attention. The story of Jesus overthrowing the money changers' tables in the Temple always puzzled Carl. He remembered seeing a rather graphic picture hanging on the wall in the fourth-grade Sunday School class at the church. Even as a ten-year-old boy, Carl had identified with something in the artist's portrayal of Christ. Now, ten years later, he felt like it was time to come to terms with his own temper. It was time to understand the force that erupted inside him and cost him so many precious relationships.

The pastor agreed to see Carl for weekly sessions for three months. Together they tried to gain insight into Carl's hostility. Their search showed why Carl was so limited in his alternatives for expressing frustration. As Carl began to trust his pastor, he shared from the depths of his isolation and fear. His pastor got a clearer picture of the internal experience of a little boy whose only role models had been violence and rejection. Carl's desperate need for love and acceptance were offset by experiences of disappointment and rejection time and time again. He was the literal product of the philosophy, "The best defense is a good offense." Fearing their parents' explosive responses, the boys—Carl and his brothers—became experts at placing blame on each other. Projecting blame was easier than accepting responsibility for their part in the family conflicts.

Carl's capacity to trust his pastor's honest and sincere support was affected greatly by the chaotic home environment from which he had come. Carl recognized that his parents were good people and that they tried hard to provide responsibly for the family, within the limits of their own capacities and resources for coping. Nevertheless, as he discovered his true feelings, Carl was disappointed that so much chaos had dominated his short, fragile life. Deep inner insecurities emerged as the pastor recognized how fragile Carl's self-esteem really was.

Analysis of the Hostile Life-Style

Carl's story is an excellent modern-day description of the biblical concept of hostility. In the Bible, hostility refers to the state of affairs between opponents or enemies who are at war with each other. The internal experience of the hostile individual, like Carl, is a state of being at war with oneself. Unable to resolve the internal war, the hostile personality frequently projects the internal conflicts upon those closest in the family, work place, or church. When we are in the presence of someone dominated by the hostile life-style, we have the continual sense that his or her anger is out of proportion to external events. Anyone is capable of experiencing occasional episodes or outbursts of frustration and anger. However, in the experience of the average person, the hostility is manageable and can be understood in light of the situation that has triggered it. Individuals like Carl are dominated by the anger they feel. They are incapable of keeping their hostility from overwhelming them and those with whom they are in relationship.

Psychologists have studied the problem of anger and hostility and have proposed many elaborate theories about this facet of human experience. The Christian confronting anger and hostility finds equally compelling arguments about the appropriateness of anger as a response between Christians. The conclusions we draw are affected also by our personal experiences, family upbringing, and individual personality dynamics. Though not all of us face the same problem of degree of hostility of someone like Carl or Saul, we nevertheless have to develop resources for coping with both our own and other people's hostilities.

A Christian psychological perspective of anger and hostility understands anger and hostility as defensive reactions against something that threatens one's sense of security. Anger can emerge whenever an individual feels anxiety or fears something threatening which must be defended against. Interestingly, each person responds to various threats differently. The same situation may cause one person to feel threatened and respond with anger while another person appears to react very quietly. Apparently, the more secure we feel, the less likely we are to use anger as a defense. Likewise, the greater the degree of threat that is experienced, the more anger will be expressed as a defense. On any given day, two different people might feel a different degree of anxiety in the face of the same threat. For that matter, the same individual might respond differently depending upon the other factors surrounding the experience of threat.

Hostility, then, as a life-style response, is a reflection of the defenses that are developed to overcome the anxieties we face. The internal conflicts that are experienced in each life situation are responded to by our defenses, including hostility. As part of those defenses, walls are erected within the internal facets of our personalities. For the hostile life-style, these defenses characteristically are angry in appearance. The hostile life-style emerges in those individuals whose lives have been so chaotic and/or violent that the defense of anger has become the immediate and characteristic response to any upsetting experience.

A Word of Hope

In Ephesians 2:14, the apostle Paul described Christ as the "peace" which breaks down the "walls of hostility." Peace within the human personality is achieved through the same medium as between external enemies. The experience of a Christ that is "peace" is an experience which negates the anxieties producing the hostility within us and around us.

Carl's early life experience made it impossible for him to understand the significance of Christ as "peace." His family life was so violent and unpredictable that he never learned to trust people or feel secure in relationships. Instead, Carl learned to expect rejection from those persons who became close to him. His father's alcoholic condition reinforced the experience of life as unpredictable and chaotic. His mother's verbally abusive relationship style challenged any belief that love could overcome problems. Carl developed an instinctive response of attack and blame whenever he felt out of control or threatened.

Even in his deepest and most important loving relationship with Sharon, Carl secretly believed he was unworthy of her love and tenderness. He was surprised by her affection and acceptance, which made him feel unsure and frightened. Carl found himself striking out at Sharon at precisely those times when she was trying to draw closer to him emotionally. His fear of her inevitable rejection and abandoning of him was so intense that he used hostility to defend himself against Sharon's closeness. Ironically, Carl discovered that he reaped rejection when he sowed hostility. The prophecy of abandonment was fulfilled, and Carl knew that he was helpless to change his attitudes and his involuntary responses by himself.

Gradually, through the counseling sessions with his pastor, Carl focused his anger at the original sources of anxiety and threat. He learned to assess accurately what kinds of situations really threatened him and what kinds of situations could be tolerated without using anger as a defense. He discovered that in many of the instances when he did feel anxiety, he could talk about it with other people, instead of needing to resort to an attacking response.

Carl learned to feel more secure within himself. The idea of Christ as "peacemaker" within him began to make sense. Through months of a patient and long-suffering ministry of his pastor, Carl experienced himself as lovable and acceptable for the first time in his life. The reality of God's love for him was only discernible after experiencing Sharon's love for him and his pastor's acceptance of him. Carl learned that love enabled him to suspend his anxious responses long enough to work out his problems with people.

As music soothed Saul, the love of friends and family soothed Carl. Now, instead of immediately aborting all relationships in which problems emerged, Carl learned to step back and work through his emotions first. Unlike Saul's reaction to David, Carl developed the ability to reach out for support and assistance to many of the people he could have chosen to fear and attack. Fortunately for Carl, he found help for his hostile life-style before it destroyed his life.

The hostile life-style is characteristic of those individuals whose anxieties overwhelm and need the aggressive and intimidating effects of hostility to protect themselves. In these individuals, the God-given emotion of anger becomes overworked at the expense of other gifts for coping with life. The angry and hostile style becomes a distorted expression of a viable human emotion and takes over the personality with both conscious and unconscious power. To a hostility-dominated individual, the world is experienced secretly as frightening and is defended against at all costs. However, as the Christ of peace intervenes upon anxieties, the need for intimidation is overcome by acceptance and openness.

5

The Sexually Seductive
Life-Style

We are bombarded with mixed messages everyday about
the subject. The television screen is filled with sexual innu-
endos, flirtations, and explicit physical encounters, whether
by advertisements, miniseries, or sporting events. Everything seems to say, "SEX!" The mixed signal from the media
has raised many questions: What is appropriate behavior or
dress? What is flirtatious? What is sinful? These questions
and more have caused many confusing and compromising
life-style situations.

The sexually seductive life-style finds its roots in more
than dirty talk or risqué apparel. The underlying causes
seem to be in reaction to male/female relationships earlier in
one's life. The reactions are not new to our day and age.
Women and men have been toying with each other in sexual
or power games since the two genders discovered each other.
The Bible records one instance even in the days of Jesus.

Character Study: The Adulterous One

In John 7:53 to 8:11 we find the account of Jesus confronted with the woman caught in adultery. One time when
Jesus had gone to the Temple to teach, a woman was
brought to Him who had been caught freely giving sexual

58

favors. The people brought her to the Temple because they wanted to hear Jesus' opinion on the subject. The whole interaction seems a bit out of place at the Temple. Jesus was there to teach, not to judge people's behavior.

Imagine all the elders of the Temple, dressed in their best clothes, gathered around Jesus. Suddenly, their discussion was interrupted by a group of men leading a woman who is obviously embarrassed and underdressed for the occasion. Her escorts leered at her as they pronounced their judgment to Jesus. "Teacher," they began, "look what we found. You know, the law says we should stone her. What do *you* think we should do?"

What a priceless moment! Imagine having the advantage of a face-to-face encounter with Jesus. Most of us have to find other avenues for healing. Take the example of the couple that follows.

Case Study: Jerry and Jean

Jerry and Jean's marriage was in real trouble. After six years, the romance was gone and both of them began to experiment with extramarital relationships. Jerry had a series of affairs with his customers at work. Since the affairs were short in duration, Jerry convinced himself that they were no real threat to his marriage with Jean. Jean suspected that Jerry was unfaithful, but chose not to confront her suspicions directly. Instead, she continued to pretend that their marriage was intact while secretly storing up years of bitterness. When her boss's wife was killed tragically in an automobile accident, he began to depend on Jean for more and more of his personal and family's daily needs. Jean found herself increasingly tempted to place herself in potentially compromising situations with him. Finally, the inevitable occurred: She succumbed to her emotional needs and began to meet him regularly for sexual relations.

In time, Jean's guilt overwhelmed her. She chose to strike out at Jerry in anger and confessed both her suspicions about his behavior and the painful truth about her own actions. Even though they had no children, something within them cried out against divorce as a quick solution to their marriage problems. Both Jean and Jerry were reared in the church. Their sexual infidelities, though, paralleled their gradual drifting away from a life-style of spiritual devotion and into a life-style characterized by increased flirtations with sexual seductive behavior. With great fear and dread, they promised to try and give their marriage another chance and sought marriage counseling with the pastor of a church different than the one in which they were members.

If you were Jerry or Jean, what would you have done? They made a good choice to see someone who was professionally trained to help them. They needed someone to help them deal with their situation as Jesus helped the woman caught in adultery.

The Response of Jesus

When Jesus was questioned by the woman's accusers, He seized the situation. Without batting an eye, Jesus asked them how they knew she was doing what they claimed she was doing. They announced that they had caught her in the very act. "Oh," said Jesus, "Then you were there?" "No," they all replied in chorus, "That is, yes, in a manner of speaking."

Jesus didn't press the point. Perhaps the accusations were

being made by some frustrated suitors. So he turned to the woman. "Why do you act this way?" asked Jesus. She didn't say much. She pulled her night gown up around her shoulders and looked around to see if there was an accepting face in the crowd. There wasn't, except for Jesus. The woman began slowly, "I guess, it makes me feel like I am somebody. For just a few moments, somebody cares for me."

Jesus grew quiet and just let the silence hang for awhile. She didn't seem to be the one with the problem. Finally, he said, "OK, let's stone her. But let's do it correctly. Let's let the man who has never done anything wrong throw the first stone. Yeah, let's let the man who has never wanted to take advantage of this woman go first." Then, Jesus dropped his eyes and apparently made some notes to give every man a chance to make a decision without His watching. When Jesus looked up again, He was alone with the woman.

So Jesus looked at her and said, "Who accuses you?" She replied, "No one." Then Jesus welcomed her and said, "Neither do I. And you know, you don't need to act this way anymore."

Analysis of the Sexually Seductive Life-Style

The pastor whom Jerry and Jean sought knew that they needed a redemptive approach, much as Jesus knew the adulterous woman needed redemption rather than death. Instead of passing quick judgment or blame, he contracted with them for several counseling sessions. He shared with them his observation that their sexual affairs and seductive life-styles seemed to be symptomatic of more than an obvious erotic attraction to members of the opposite sex. In the pastor's opinion, their seductive behavior was a reflection of their hidden fears of unworthiness. After some thought, both Jerry and Jean admitted that they did feel unworthy, and in fact those feelings predated their marriage.

Jerry acknowledged a lifelong preoccupation with chasing women and recalled how he had been "unfaithful" to many of his girl friends prior to meeting Jean. He also confessed that even one month prior to their wedding, he spent the night with a woman on a business trip in another city. Though not as overt as Jerry, Jean's confessions revealed a history of flirtatious encounters with men. Since puberty, she was aware that her body had power to influence men and to get them to respond to her needs for attention and affirmation. Furthermore, Jean revealed that she always had been infatuated with men other than her husband. Now she was realizing that what she called her "affairs of the heart" were in many ways more dangerous than her sexual affair with her boss. She was looking for ways to feel wanted or accepted. The harmless flirtations led to the eventual affair with her boss.

Under the skillful direction of the pastor, Jean and Jerry began to realize that they had seduced themselves into a quick-fix solution in much the same way as the woman caught in adultery had done. Jerry and Jean were using emotional satisfaction of sexual affirmation to respond to the deep questions of self-esteem and anxiety. Jerry understood how he had used sexuality to express anger and control with women. He wondered if this were a reaction to some early traumatic experiences with female authorities in his life. He remembered vividly how he felt mistreated by his first-grade teacher. She repeatedly embarrassed him in front of the class by making him read aloud, knowing full well that he would stumble over the difficult words. He confessed that he never felt comfortable with women and that he overcame that anxiety through sexual conquest.

Jean connected her addiction to "affairs of the heart" as a life-style attempt to compensate for never feeling accepted, loved, or appreciated in a male-dominated family. Her father and brother were set apart as "overlords" while she and her mother catered to their every whim. Even the tastiest meal the women prepared was treated as a meager offering. Feeling worthless, powerless, and insignificant to her favorite men, Jean went looking for her self-affirmation with any male who would respond to her sexuality with positive affirmation.

Jean and Jerry had merged their sexual needs with their spiritual needs as well. Jean recalled an early awareness of how much sexuality was expressed in disguise in her home church. She recalled several experiences of confusion as a teenager in which many of the men at church, including her pastor, gave her conflicting messages about her femaleness. On the one hand, she was subjected to continual intense sermons, Sunday School lessons, and youth devotional experiences which were clearly designed to raise her anxiety about the sinful potential of sexual behavior. On the other hand, many of these same individuals would not hesitate to greet her with hugs and kisses, all done "in the spirit of Christian brotherly love." Needing the affirmation that came with the hugs and kisses, she recalled trying to ignore the conflict that this behavior had caused her. Jerry laughed and also acknowledged that he had joined right in with this seductive behavior, but with a more honest awareness of what he gained in the way of erotic satisfaction wrapped in the sheep's clothing of "brotherly love."

Jerry and Jean discovered the extent that they had attempted to resolve their inner conflicts of self-worth and esteem through the use of sexually seductive behaviors. The immediate gratification found in an erotic and emotional affirmation in a sexual encounter was soon replaced with a deeper anxiety and fear. "What will happen if my sexual charms fade with age?" became the question after each encounter. When another opportunity appeared to use the same strategy to postpone the anxiety, they succumbed to sexually seductive behavior, only to have their fears return again. It was a vicious cycle, repeating over and over. Feeling unworthy led to sex, which led to feeling unworthy, and so on. "Sometimes I think I am addicted to sex," lamented Jerry. "Will anyone notice me if I don't play the sexual games?" questioned Jean.

The life-style of sexual seduction becomes a distortion of the natural and God-given enjoyment of our sexuality. Since sexual experiences have intense emotional and physical responses, the seductive life-style uses this power to respond to the anxiety of low self-esteem, advancing age, and fears of losing attractiveness. This distorts the concept that God created us as sexual beings with the blessing of enjoying each other as such. Seductive behavior ignores the constraints which allow for the proper context of sexuality. The affirmation and wholeness expressed by a husband and wife in their sexual experience is a reflection of a shared history of daily experiences of similar expressions of affirmation and wholeness. The co-raising of children, the joint task of household chores, the sharing of dreams and aspirations lead to wonderfully fulfilling sexual responses. Without a history of shared affirming experiences, sexuality is reduced to coexistent bodily functions.

Jean and Jerry wept as they realized the truth in the pastor's words. They had allowed their marriage to be merely coexistence, refusing to share with each other. They had failed to learn while becoming adults how to care for themselves, much less to care for others. Neither felt any self-worth, so neither could treat others as having worth. They could only use personal relationships to passify their fears of unworthiness.

A Word of Hope

The pastor advised Jerry and Jean to begin a process of practicing affirmation with each other. Following the example of Jesus and the adulterous woman, Jerry would daily welcome Jean, to accept her as a worthy person without expecting anything from her. Through a set of structured exercises, Jerry would help Jean realize her own worth, to feel comfortable with herself without needing male approval. These exercises included things such as regular times for sharing of thoughts and hopes, the giving of compliments for Jean's gifts and strengths, dating experiences with each other, and spontaneous gift giving. The terms *practice* and *exercise* were used because, at first, Jerry would have to make an effort to do things with his wife. In time, though, these "exercises" would become second nature. To similarly help Jerry, Jean was to follow a similar pattern of behavior.

The solution to Jerry's and Jean's life-style problems was not easy. Each needed to accept him- or herself out of a realization that they were children of God, and, by virtue of that relationship, they had worth. That is to say, regardless of appearances or sexual attractiveness, each of them had worth simply because God had created them. Jesus welcomed the adulterous woman, not because He was sexually attracted to her or because He wanted anything from her.

Jesus welcomed her because she was human, like Himself, and had feelings, desires, and hopes. She needed to live in relationship with others without fearing what they might expect or want from her or whether her effort would be deemed worthy.

In the case of Jean and Jerry, after understanding their worth from God's perspective, they could grow in their understanding of self-acceptance and worth in each other's eyes. By daily giving and sharing with each other, in time, their needs to seek sexual satisfaction outside of their marriage could be overcome. This is not to say that the desire for extramarital affairs would disappear, though it might. This is to say that a shared growing experience of self-worth in an understanding of the grace of God's acceptance in Jesus Christ proves more powerful than the desire for sexual gratification. If God has welcomed us in Jesus, then our feelings of worth have found the greatest level of acceptance.

6

The Controlling Life-Style

One of the funniest movies I have seen is *Vacation*, starring Chevy Chase. The movie strikes such a chord within me that I start laughing before the next scene even starts. I remember well a scene where Chase is mapping out their vacation for his family on their home computer. Situated against a backdrop of a map of the United States, Chase guides a little car across the country, giving intricate detail to what will be fun and how long they will enjoy that fun. The children, caring little about being told when to have fun, begin to entertain themselves on the computer screen. As the family car moves along the vacation path, the children guide gobbling "Pacmen" and shooting spaceships after it. Yes, the scene reminded me of some of my family's vacations when my parents mapped out fun for me, not realizing that I would miss the fun in the rigidness of the structure.

Structure is not bad. We all need a level of order in our lives to help us cope with the anxiety of unanswered questions and unseen futures. Tending to have a rigid control over life is what leads to the controlling life-style. Needing to have every moment or movement carefully mapped out beforehand will lead to a dictatorial perspective on life.

This type of perspective denies the belief in the sovereignty of God and faith in God's goodness to seek justice.

The Bible may not offer specific illustrations of the controlling life-style, but it does give clear examples of God's sovereignty. One such example might be Jonah. We are familiar with Jonah's conflict with the big fish, but listen again to an underlying conflict in Jonah's life.

Character Study: Jonah

Jonah was fuming. Nothing was going according to the plan. He had done his part; now God wasn't doing what Jonah expected. Jonah had gone through the whole ordeal of going to Nineveh, even though he didn't want to. The round-about trip to Nineveh had been no holiday. Anything could have gone wrong, and most of it did. A little rickety boat, a raging tempest at sea, swimming in the angry waves, and three turbulent days in a fish belly are not the sorts of things one shares slides of with friends. God had told Jonah to go preach Nineveh's destruction. Jonah had gone to Nineveh and preached. Nineveh was full of wickedness that God wouldn't tolerate anymore. Nineveh's days definitely were numbered. The Ninevites had repented, but Jonah still wanted them to be punished. Jonah almost relished the thought. He was enjoying this so much, he might have fantasized that he should be allowed to push the button which would rain down the fire and brimstone on the evil city of Nineveh.

When God didn't destroy Nineveh, Jonah became disillusioned. He felt like God had been unfaithful to him, allowing him to appear like a foolish doomsday fanatic. The situation was out of control and not proceeding according to plan. Jonah was angry. He never had been made to feel so foolish before, and Jonah needed someone to vent his anger upon. Jonah stalked out of the city, made a booth for himself, and sat down to wait and see what would happen to the city. But sitting in the sun only made Jonah hotter under the collar.

As Jonah baked, a castor oil plant grew up over him, providing shade from the heat. Jonah must have laughed. When Jonah was a little boy and had gotten this angry, his mother had ground up this plant's pods, squeezed out the oil, and made Jonah drink an ounce. She said it would lighten his load and sweeten his disposition. Jonah didn't know whether his disposition had ever been affected, though he knew castor oil was a laxative. At this moment in his life, Jonah was preoccupied with his embarrassment and anger. How ironic it seems that of all the plants and trees that God could have allowed to grow in that precise spot, here was that familiar reminder of the catharsis he needed.

The plant grew taller, spread its leaves, then attracted a worm which ate the insides out, causing the plant to wither and eventually die. Jonah just blew up. He had needed that plant. He had needed Nineveh to be destroyed. Things had to go as he planned. Specific actions led to specific results. Jonah had structured his whole life around that premise. Nineveh had been wicked. God had promised that wickedness would be destroyed. Therefore, Nineveh should be destroyed. Jonah was getting pretty upset with what appeared to be God's unreliability. Now, in the middle of the day's intense heat, that plant had died, just when he had needed it most.

Case Study: Harold

Jonah wished to see himself in ultimate control. He

wanted to give the orders and watch his requests become reality. Unbeknown to himself, Harold was such a person also. When relationships with his three children fractured, Harold realized this.

When Harold and his wife, Shirley, walked into the pastor's study that Wednesday evening, the pastor figured the problem was their daughter. The pastor was well aware of the family's problems with the two older boys. Harold, Jr., had dropped out of college and joined the armed forces. Peter had just recently been hospitalized for drug and alcohol abuse. These two children had given the forty-five-year-old president of a family-owned business and his bookkeeper wife enough heartache for a lifetime. Now it seems that their unmarried nineteen-year-old daughter, Tina, was to have a baby.

The pastor was equipped to refer them to the various social agencies in the area, including a fine denominationally sponsored home for unwed mothers in a neighboring city. However, the pastor's real concern went deeper than finding a solution to the immediate problem of Tina's pregnancy. He knew that Harold would be very hard to deal with in this situation, as he had been in the previous instances involving the two sons. Harold responded to every personal crisis with the same strategies that he used in business. Harold believed that the answer to any problem involved a thorough analysis of the "facts," followed by the correct and efficient implementation of a logical solution.

Harold is a fine man, a responsible member of church and community, and an excellent provider for his family's material needs. He has served as treasurer of the church for the last decade and as a trustee of the church as well. His performance is above reproach and professional in every detail.

The pastor had noted on several occasions, though, that when challenged by other parishioners whose perspectives were different from his, Harold became very authoritarian and inflexible in his response. His inflexibility would then aggravate the situation by offending other people who could not tolerate his insensitivity to their feelings.

The pastor had seen problems developing with Harold's children for years. They were all three good kids, but they consistently found themselves at odds with their father. Whenever they differed from their father's opinions and beliefs, Harold responded in that same tightly structured way that he did in the other critical situations of his life. Harold's adeptness for organization and for providing sturcture appeared to be the very same force that drove his children and fellow parishioners away from him. Furthermore, it was impossible to get Harold to see how the feelings of the other persons could be affecting the outcome of the crises.

Shirley had confided to the pastor's wife on several occasions of her fear that Harold was driving his children out of the home with his "dictatorial" style. She felt helpless when she tried to get him to soften his approach with the children.

Tina's untimely pregnancy seemed to highlight the futility of Harold's controlling style. By her actions, she had communicated clearly that her feelings and passions ran deeper than his efforts to get her and her brothers to conform to his wishes and beliefs. The father of the baby wasn't even someone that she was seriously committed to emotionally, so her condition seemed to be directed more toward her conflicts with her father than with her own desires to find intimacy with a lover her own age.

Harold surprised the pastor with an uncharacteristic reflection: "I feel like such a failure. All three of my precious children have disappointed me so. It almost seems that they are trying to tell me something! Do you suppose I have missed something important in the way I have related to them?" he questioned.

The pastor sensed the opening he had been waiting for and used the questioning responses of Harold as the opportunity to encourage Harold's reflection upon the strengths and weaknesses of his controlling life-style. Harold shared how his fears about being out of control had plagued him his whole life. He recalled a deeply painful experience of losing control of his emotions and crying in the first grade in front of the entire class. He vowed never to let his emotions rule his behavior again. His role model for manliness became his stoic, puritanical grandfather. He developed a rational problem-solving approach for conflict from that point forward. His wife's emotionality had always troubled Harold, and his sense of responsibility as a parent had led him to try and teach his sons what they would need to be successful men as well. He had interpreted their resistance to his teaching as typical rebellion. Only now was it dawning on him that his children were rebelling against his style more than against him.

When did the truth become apparent on Jonah? After the tree had withered, God spoke to Jonah. "Jonah, why are you so upset?" Jonah snapped, "Lord, you know why I'm mad. We made a deal. I would go to Nineveh and preach to them about the plans for their destruction. Now that I have succeeded in frightening them into repentance, You've backed out on Your plans. Nineveh is still standing. And now that plant has abandoned me too, leaving me out here in the sun to wither as well." So God replied, "Come on,

Jonah. That's not it at all. That's not why you are so mad. You're mad because you just figured out that you can't control any of it—not the trip, not Nineveh's condition, not life, not even the plant. That scares you, Jonah, because life doesn't react to your wishes or premises. You can't be in control. That's My responsibility. And if I choose to be gracious with Nineveh or this plant, you do well to enjoy that grace also."

Analysis of the Controlling Life-Style

The characteristics of the controlling life-style are well represented by Harold and by our interpretation of Jonah. When confronted with anxious experiences, one frequent response is to bind one's anxieties and feelings and to seek a structured, logical response. Anxiety and fear often overwhelm an individual, amplifying feelings and making them unable to face life. The embarrassment or shame one feels in the face of losing control, magnified by others' witness to that loss of control, further aggravate the experience. Instead of losing control, the choice of a logical and structured problem-solving method is embraced gratefully.

Shame, the feeling of embarrassment or exposure or feeling as though one doesn't measure up to a standard of behavior is a common early childhood experience. Shame is also a primitive and painful emotion that can be experienced throughout life. Shame dominates the young child who is learning to be toilet trained. In an effort to please the parents, the child must exhibit self-control as quickly as possible. Toilet training is not the only childhood experience by which a child might feel shame in the presence of the parent. In any instance where the child feels his or her performance is less than desired, the child experiences shame. In fact, any authority figure can elict the shame emotion in a child who feels substandard in performance. Teachers, ministers, grandparents, older respected siblings, or supervisors can affect a child in this same way.

Harold reported to his pastor how ashamed he had felt when he cried in elementary school. He reflected that his grandfather was an important example for him on how to avoid any future similar experiences. Grandpa's strategy of self-discipline and careful planning not only helped avoid shameful losses of control but rewarded Harold in school and work performance as well. Like most individuals with life-style strategies, Harold applied his controlling style to every aspect of his life indiscriminately. Any emotion which he could not understand, Harold equated with shame. Harold eventually decided that all emotions were to be guarded against. That meant that even positive emotions such as love, joy, and happiness or healthy emotions such as grief were restricted by Harold's tight control. Any emotion which Harold experienced fell under the control of his strategy, leaving him more like an unfeeling computer than a vibrant human being.

Harold's controlling life-style continued a step further. The same strict requirements which Harold applied to himself were expected from all others around him. His family, his employees, and his fellow parishioners were pained by Harold's control which dominated their relationships with him. His family retreated from him whenever they suspected they might trigger Harold's shame-induced controlling life-style. The home was reduced to a place where only factual or logical information was shared. Shirley became less spontaneous and open with Harold, growing less tender toward Harold in time. The children lost sight of Harold as a support figure because they were frustrated by his demanding qualities. When Harold tried to structure family events to grow closer, the family balked at the structure and lack of spontaneity of the events. Even his wife could not respond romantically to Harold's tightly controlled initiatives.

Each child in turn tried to allow the family to be more flexible and for Harold to loosen his controlling style. Harold, Jr., confronted his dad's plans for his future by dropping out of college and heading in his own direction toward a military career. Peter cried out for help and attention by becoming involved with drugs. Now Tina sought affection from her father through sexual involvement with a boyfriend and the eventual pregnancy.

A Word of Hope

The story of Jonah was chosen and interpreted as a biblical illustration of the implications of the controlling lifestyle. Jonah's experience provides a helpful spiritual insight into the core problems within the controlling style. The final consequence of Jonah's efforts to deny the sovereignty of God by falsely elevating his own decisions above God's produced a tragic separation from God. Like Harold, Jonah needed to have everyone's life conform to his priorities and expectations. Like Harold, Jonah judged his contemporaries as inadequate to such an extent that Jonah ultimately was guilty of judging God as well. Jonah attempted not only to control his own destiny but wanted to control the destiny of a whole city as well. In attempting to expand the influence of his control beyond his own life, Jonah was guilty of sinning against God. Jonah wanted to usurp God's sovereign right to judge or be gracious.

The sad consequence of the controlling life-style is the inability to be open to personal, relational, and spiritual moments of grace. Grace by nature is not logical or structured. Grace is free, undeserving, and spontaneous, both in the offering and the receiving. The experience of grace can be so overwhelming that intense feelings such as gratitude, joy, forgiveness, and peace occur without plan, structure, or control. A controlling individual like Harold is so well defended against nonrational experiences that even the ultimate healing power of grace is defended against.

The experience of shame, which lies at the root of the controlling life-style, needs grace and acceptance to be transformed. The acceptance of one's humanity erases the experience of shame. Unfortunately, the same defenses which protected against shame and produced the controlling life-style also filter out the opportunity to accept one's humanity. The self-imposed sovereignty of a Jonah or a Harold keeps the person from receiving the blessing of acceptance by another. Similarly, such a person has difficulty embracing God's loving acceptance and grace.

Harold sensed how self-defeating his strategy had become. Through his children's initiative and with his wife's support, he finally reached out to his pastor for help. The pastor led him toward overcoming his self-defeating lifestyle. With his pastor's assistance, Harold understood the dynamics of his life-style and learned the important spiritual lesson taught by Jonah. He talked with his pastor about the many life experiences of anxiety about not measuring up, not performing adequately, and of feeling shameful. He was relieved to find that these conversations were helpful in allowing him to experience the full intensity of these emotions without the self-constructed shelter of his controlling style. Like Jonah, exposed without his castor oil plant to hide him from the consequences of his own harsh judgments, Harold began to experience the acceptance of both his own and others' limitations. His pastor, his wife, and his children taught Harold how much freedom could be his to experience as he loosened up and let God take final control of his destiny.

7

The Handicapped Life-Style

Case Study: Arnold

Arnold is a fifty-two-year-old resident at a rehabilitation center. He has been living at the rehab center for the last four years since a motorcycle accident left him paralyzed from the waist down. Arnold is recently divorced from Sally and described the divorce to the chaplain as a direct outcome of his accident and disability. He is currently unemployed and receiving disability income while working on vocational rehabilitation in the training program at the rehab center.

The chaplain was aware of Arnold and noticed his lack of cooperation with many of the programs and structures that had been designed to meet his particular needs. Arnold was quite angry and had adopted the-world-owes-me-a-living philosophy of life that had undermined the rehab treatment plan of getting him to take responsibility for his future. Since many of Arnold's statements about his anger were couched in religious terms and reflected that Arnold felt some anger toward God, the chaplain wished to develop a counseling relationship with Arnold to see if something could be done to change his attitude and lift his morale.

Arnold immediately agreed to see the chaplain and enjoyed the weekly opportunities to vent his frustration and to complain about his life situation. His interpretation of his wife leaving him put the entire responsibility on her and blamed his disability for having eliminated their fast-paced life-style. The chaplain later interviewed Arnold's ex-wife and discovered that his disability had not destroyed their relationship, but his bitterness, passivity, and irresponsibility had become unbearable to her.

Apparently Arnold had grown accustomed to the sympathy and uncomfortableness that other people felt in the face of his disability and their wholeness of body. He learned how to capitalize on the other person's guilt and anxiety. For the first few months of his rehabilitation, these feelings had been managed by the treatment team with the hope that Arnold would soon grow out of his need to capitalize upon his handicap to avoid taking any responsibility for his own future. Arnold had managed to get into conflicts with several residents at the rehab facility as a result of his excuses over not being able to fulfill his designated duties around the dormitory and work placement areas. Several more physically incapacitated residents became angry at Arnold's unwillingness to perform the rather simple and manageable tasks that the group had decided together he was capable of doing.

The chaplain soon noted Arnold's tendencies to get him to try to run errands, make phone calls, or secure assistance in projects that Arnold was quite capable of doing for himself. When the chaplain confronted Arnold, he was then exposed to the full fury of Arnold's anger with unfounded accusations of his "insensitivity, lack of compassion, and unprofessional conduct." Every effort to get Arnold to see the ways that he had managed to turn his handicap into a convenience for his passivity and dependence were met with great resistance. On several occasions, the chaplain overheard Arnold make disparaging remarks to other residents about the chaplain's insensitivity and lack of professionalism. Arnold then denied having made these comments when he was confronted later in the counseling session by the chaplain.

Arnold's hopes were centered on getting the rehabilitation services to purchase him a specially outfitted van. With the van, Arnold could drive himself about and secure a white-collar job in a local radio station. Arnold turned down several job opportunities because they were beneath his idea of a salary or status that he was worth or the job required him to retrain and develop skills that Arnold saw as demeaning to himself. The situation progressed to such a degree that the social worker confessed to the chaplain that she quit trying to find adequate vocational placement for Arnold. He almost always ended up embarrassing her with the inappropriate way in which he would handle the interviews and eventually declined whatever offer had been made.

Arnold's story is remarkably similar to the biblical account of the paralytic man brought to Jesus for healing by his four dependable friends. Allowing for some imagination, let's consider these similarities.

Character Study: The Lame One

The story is found in the fifth chapter of Luke. Without specifics being given, there is ample evidence that these men were lifelong friends. To them, life's challenges were a game, and four finer players or friends could not be found in the world. We don't know their names or the name of their paralytic friend, but no reader can miss the extent of their care for him. They carried him to Jesus, they crawled up on the roof, and they lowered their friend to the Master. Was there no limit to their friendship? We can imagine that they always did things together. No request was too great, even as they carried the paralytic on their shoulders, they made it seem more like an adventure than a chore. What was the difference? They had carried him in one way or another all of his life.

Yes, they were good friends. The paralytic remembered what his childhood had been like. It seemed that little group of five had always been together. They were always playing and teasing each other or spending the night at each other's houses. There was always something to do that seemed to be full of fun. Even that one awful winter, they were together. Who could forget the sickness, that nagging cough that never went away and only lingered on and on? Or the sense of weakness in his legs, and how that weakness spread like numbing cold up his back? It wasn't long until he felt useless, just good enough for the scrap heap. His four friends, though, never gave up on him. Sure there were some kidding and lost tempers now and then. Everybody is human. But the hard work from his friends in seeing to his every need allowed the paralytic to survive.

No doubt his childhood had been difficult. The tendency would be to baby him constantly, to see to his every whim. Surely, the handicapped youth used this to his advantage as well and developed quite a chip on his shoulder. He was the first to lay guilt on others about his handicap. He was the last to admit to anyone that he was helpless without them, both physically and emotionally. He was dependent on others to make his decisions, to take him places, and to care for him in general. It wasn't easy, and at times, the situation could get everybody down. On exceptionally bad days, after some anger and guilt had been spread around, everyone felt crippled.

Now, here they were, on the road to see Jesus. The news had traveled that Jesus was a miracle worker. Folk were regaining sight, being cured of leprosy, and the lame were walking. Yes, the lame were walking. Well, this is what the doctor ordered. The paralytic admitted that he was a little skeptical about the whole thing, but his four buddies talked him into at least trying it. So they had begun the journey to Jesus.

When they arrived at the house where Jesus was healing people on that particular day, there was quite a sight. A thousand people seemed to be crowding into one tiny house. From a distance, it didn't look like they had much of a chance to get close to the place, much less to get in. Sensing the problem in getting their paralyzed friend in to see Jesus, the four young men decided to enter the building through the roof. Now the paralytic was scared. He didn't like the idea of going up on the roof. He certainly was in no condition to climb, and he didn't like the idea of being a spectacle. The more he considered all of the risks involved, the more he disliked the whole idea. He didn't want to be healed *that much*. But it was out of his hands, so to speak.

His friends gave him a pep talk, they all touched him, and then they pulled and scraped and clawed his body up onto the roof. Unlike today, this roof wasn't made of pine and plaster, but mud and straw. The friends quickly made a hole in the roof and lowered their paralytic friend to the feet of Jesus. There he was, as useless as the roof through which he had just been lowered.

Jesus looked at the paralytic and said, "Your sins are forgiven." The paralytic probably was so embarrassed and angry, he might have said, "Man, are you crazy? I haven't done anything wrong. You think I made this happen to me? Like I was careless or something? I'm sick! I'm sick! I'm not bad." Jesus knew differently, though. Jesus knew about the anger, the spite, the pride, the guilt, the fear—even that fear right up to a moment ago. The comment by Jesus about sins doesn't seem so inappropriate in that context. It is as if Jesus might have said, "You think you are the only one in the world with a handicap? That's not your problem. Not being able to walk has never stopped you from being the person you were intended to be. But I'll tell what has—all this anger and selfishness of yours is your real handicap. Your sin in allowing these things to dominate you is the problem. You can't even lift your own finger without help. Well, let go of your problems. Let them go. Your sins no longer bind you. You're free!"

The paralytic responded to Jesus' invitation. The Bible doesn't tell us anything else about him. Only that he stood up, took his belongings, and went on his way. He realized that his paralysis was not limited to his legs. His emotions and spirit also had been paralyzed. In that moment, he came face-to-face with the full nature of his condition. He recognized how his life-style had been characterized by preoccupation with not being able to walk. He had forgotten how to live. In that encounter with Jesus, he was able to forgive himself, his family, his friends, and perhaps, even God.

Analysis of the Handicapped Life-Style

Handicapped individuals face tremendous challenges in life that the sighted, hearing, ambulatory, or speaking members of society frequently take for granted. To be born without all of one's natural resources for living, or to have a portion of them suddenly taken by illness or accident, is a significant liability even in today's high-tech society. For many handicapped persons, the forced dependency on family, friends, social agencies, and a variety of artificial appliances is demoralizing. To choose to lean upon the care of others is a challenge to one's self-image and self-esteem. To have this dependency forced upon us for survival without our choice is even more complex. The accompanying emotions of anger, grief, guilt, and shame are understandable, but no less easy to manage.

As with Arnold, the primary relationships with members of one's own family frequently are hardest. To be ultimately dependent upon a spouse, child, or parent can elicit an abundance of rage that eventually overwhelms any relationship. Divorce and/or abandonment to social agencies is a tempting alternative to the parent or spouse who cannot adjust to both the physical disabilities and the personality changes.

The handicapped individual adopts a handicapped life-style. The handicapped life-style is one where a handicap dominates every value or consideration of life. Life is defined exclusively by the handicap and is consumed by a self-image of being inadequate or flawed. Aspects of one's personhood not related to the specific handicap are, never-theless, undeveloped because of the false belief that there are no potential strengths. Because of his bitterness, Arnold withdrew from opportunities to develop skills that he could have mastered. He believed that his life was not worth the investment since he was not completely whole. Arnold could have learned a marketable skill, but he did not apply himself toward learning because he was so angry and felt the world owed him a living.

A Word of Hope

Those who have successfully rehabilitated themselves say that a part of the process of rehabilitation involved accept-ing the realistic limitations that the handicap placed on their lives. That is to say, to overcome the handicapped life-style, an individual needs to understand the reality of his or her condition. There are limitations to life, but life is not over. Some persons fail to work through this stage of denial effectively. They place themselves in situations of impossible difficulty rather than accept the alternatives that might en-courage their success. They do not want to succeed if the success requires their acceptance of help from others.

The spiritual issues of pride/humility are evident in the handicapped life-style. Excessive pride can produce an atti-tude of arrogant defiance on the one hand or an equally dis-abling attitude of passivity on the other hand. The spirit of genuine humility, evidenced by the healed paralytic in the biblical story, enables a handicapped individual to release the destructive power of pent-up rage and bitterness and to move forward in maximizing his or her quality of life.

Overcoming the handicapped life-style begins with realizing the limitations of one's conditions and developing new or redefined expectations for a meaningful life. These new expectations include the allowance for others to help with limitations. The greatest humility is to admit one needs help and to accept that help from others. God's grace is offered to us all in Jesus Christ, but that grace is felt most tangibly in the assistance of a person who cares for us. The paralytic in Luke received two gifts of grace. The first was Jesus' assurance that the man's sins were forgiven, and the second was the daily help he had from his friends.

8

The Despairing Life-Style

Depression is a common human experience. Depression can affect everything you do—the way you dress, the way you talk, even the way you look. A humorous example of this type of depression was depicted on the television series, "The Cosby Show." One of the daughters, Vanessa, had to attend a family outing instead of going to a party with her friends. For the duration of the show, Vanessa moped through the house, dressed in her bathrobe and gloomy face, completely oblivious to the rest of the family's activities. Finally, her father confronted Vanessa, telling her that enough was enough and that, beginning the next day, Vanessa should put on a smiling face and go on with life. This is one example of depression—moping around in a bathrobe, gloomy faced, and disenchanted with life. Depression in the more extreme forms feels endless, bottomless, and hopeless. This kind of depression (that is, endless, bottomless, and hopeless) affects the entire person—body, mind, and spirit. The continual presence of an extreme level of depression is a major factor leading to a life-style of despair.

Television isn't the only medium for examples of depression. The Bible, too, has examples of physically and emotionally draining times that occur when something which was really wanted is no longer possible. There are a variety of biblical pictures of depression. Of these pictures of depression, those where physical symptoms are present, such as a downcast facial expression, typify that type of depression which permeates one's being to the extent that the human body cannot help but reflect the level of hopelessness and despair.

Character Study: The Disciples on the Road to Emmaus

LK 24:13 - 35

A classic New Testament picture of depression and despair is found in Luke 24. Two disciples were going from Jerusalem to Emmaus. It was a dark journey, not because the sun wasn't shining but because of the events of the past few days. The two travelers had been followers and witnesses of the life and works of Jesus. Unfortunately they also had witnessed His tragic death on a cross. That had been a dark day; even the sun had hidden behind the gloomy covering of clouds. Perhaps no darker day has occurred in human existence. Jesus, who had represented all of their hopes for the future, had been taken from them. Their dreams of a new Israel, their hope, was gone. They were in despair, and their faces reflected the depth of their loss. *A Lost Cause.* The biblical term used here describes one whose face is darkened or downcast because of a sad experience. The face of the depressed one betrays the hurt of a hope-drained spirit. The same term is used in some classical writings to refer to a particular river upon whose banks a soldier learns of his son's death. You can imagine the picture—waiting for your ship to come in, then being gripped with the news that your child was killed. As any parent can attest, children provide a window to the future, a link from one's past leading toward what one hopes will be. That is depression or despair—having one's future or hope ripped away.

Daily life adjustments can bring about depressive feelings. Extended and uninterrupted depression will frequently culminate in despair. Depression can result from a natural life change, such as a child leaving home. Sometimes feelings which are identified as depression also characterize despair. In fact, often what is perceived as depression is only the surface evidence of an underlying state of despair. Depression can become despair when a series of depressing events yield a continual condition of sadness, anxiety, and hopelessness.

Case Study: Amy

Amy had been battling with depression over a number of incidents for years. When her older daughter, Karen, left for college, the depression forced Amy to seek professional help again. Amy had been under the care of a psychiatrist for five years, since the death of her mother. The recent separation from Calvin, her husband of twenty-five years, and Karen's leaving home led Amy to believe that even her psychiatrist's antidepressants and electroshock treatments would not be enough to relieve the pain.

Amy began to wonder if her problem had not become a spiritual problem as well. She, therefore, accepted her pastor's suggestion that a pastoral counselor be consulted. In reviewing Amy's situation with the psychiatrist, the pastoral counselor agreed that Amy's depression seemed to have the added spiritual component of despair.

Despair is the loss of hope. Though similar to depression in the presence of clear changes in the emotional state of the individual, despair reflects a significant change in the person's spiritual health as well. The counselor discovered that shortly after the death of her mother, Amy began to become irregular in her church attendance and described a growing sense of frustration in her personal spiritual disciplines of prayer and Bible study.

Amy described a lifelong struggle to feel accepted by others, especially her mother. She indicated that she was the product of a broken home; her father divorced her mother when Amy was three years old. Amy's mother turned all of her emotional energy into raising Amy. Mother and daughter were inseparable.

Amy did well in public school and received a scholarship to attend college. She decided to save money and commuted to the college while staying at her mother's house. During her junior year of college, Amy met Calvin, fell in love, and got pregnant. She and Calvin got married shortly thereafter, but she miscarried on their honeymoon. Amy reported that she believed God had punished her for her premarital sexual activity with Calvin and had taken the baby as payment for that indiscretion. Amy's mother had been very disappointed over the pregnancy, but she had supported the marriage to prevent a scandal in their small hometown. Nevertheless, Amy's mother had frequently made negative comments to Amy that reflected how disappointed she was in Amy's premarital behavior. Amy had vowed that she would regain her mother's confidence if it took the rest of her life.

After Amy's mother became a semi-invalid by a stroke, Amy and Calvin took her into their home, so Amy could provide constant nursing care. The counselor realized that

Amy had brought her mother into her home when Karen was three years old and immediately before Amy gave birth to a second daughter. Amy had assumed primary responsibility for an infant, an invalid mother, and a three-year-old child all within a year's time. Slowly, Amy realized that her depression was an understandable result of the extraordinary stresses in her life. She and Calvin had argued and debated about the quality of their marriage for most of the last fifteen years. Calvin had always complained that when Amy got through taking care of her mother and her two daughters, she had little time—and no emotional energy—left for him!

Amy never felt released from the curse of her premarital indiscretion. She reported that she never reestablished the level of trust and intimacy with her mother that had existed before she met Calvin. Nothing that she did, not even her loyal nursing of her mother at the expense of her marriage or her own health, undid the pain of that breach in their relationship.

When her mother died, Amy felt abandoned by God as well. She no longer had any hope of being reconciled to her mother or regaining the emotional blessing which had been lost. Her guilt and shame forever were exposed in her own mind and heart, and no absolution could be received now that her mother was no longer alive to be cared for.

Karen's leaving home for college seemed to repeat the feelings of rejection and abandonment for Amy. She was unable to serve her mother or her husband, and now her daughter was gone as well. With these primary relationships missing, Amy had no one to work out her need for acceptance. She only could conclude that God had abandoned her too. Maybe she really was unacceptable to God as her mother had communicated to her.

Analysis of the Despairing Life-Style

Amy's example provides several evidences of how the losses of life affect us emotionally, physically, and spiritually. Amy continued to live under the compound sadness of losing her mother's confidence and trust, her personal sense of integrity, her miscarriage, her mother's physical presence after the stroke and eventual death, her marriage with Calvin, and her daughter's leaving home. To experience any loss by reacting with sadness and mourning is to respond to the realities of life with the appropriate emotions which the Lord has given us. We are provided opportunities to express these emotions within the supportive care of family, friends, and church with the hope that as these feelings of grief and loss are expressed, we can eventually feel relieved of the burden of our losses.

The compound nature of Amy's condition provided no avenue of relief to her grief and loss. She became "acquainted with grief" in such a familiar way that depression became a way of living for her entire adult life. All of her relationships were colored by the darkness of her troubled heart. Added to that was the burden of her reoccurring fear that she might lose something she cherished.

Amy was despairing, as well as depressed, and she gradually lost hope that her future would ever be brighter than her present. She felt no awareness of God's presence and loving care for her. Having lost her integrity in both her own and her mother's eyes, she suffered the daily torment of believing that she must devote her entire life to finding forgiveness for an act which could not be undone. Her mother's judgment seized her own heart and left no room for a loving Lord to provide her with an experience of grace and forgiveness.

Aspects of Amy's condition are surprisingly common. We internalize our experiences of our parents' acceptance or disapproval of us and emerge from those experiences believing that God's response to us must be identical! The moments of grace that remind us of God's continuing presence and love are hard to measure in the same tangible ways that a parent's forgiveness and acceptance can be felt. An obvious frown changing to a smile or rejection replaced by an embrace can help to alleviate the pain of our wrongdoing and our guilt and shame. And yet, parent-child relationships are sometimes so fragile that the much-needed resolution to these painful experiences cannot be shared together.

Amy never was able to distinguish between her mother's angry rejection and God's response of forgiveness. She spent her adult life trying to undo the consequences of her impulsive sexual encounter with Calvin and the loss of a baby never born. She unfairly blamed herself for that miscarriage and participated in a miscarriage of judgment over her entire life! Her mother's inability to forgive her and restore her self-worth became fused within Amy as evidence that God would not acknowledge her sincere penance and give her a second chance. Without the prospect of a second chance, Amy's grief moved into depression, became colored with the feeling of hopelessness, and captured her personality as despair.

Amy wanted to restore the essence of a perfect parent-child relationship in her own overinvestment in Karen. She tried to love Karen in the way that she wanted her mother to love her. Karen's impending graduation and moving away to attend college in another state provided an opportunity for the familiar feelings of abandonment from the "Garden of Eden" to arise again within Amy.

One of the most hopeless feelings that we can experience is the belief that we can never receive the love and attention that we need to survive and thrive. Many individuals function as if there were not enough love in the world around them for everyone to receive what he or she needs. In the absence of enough love and attention, these necessities of life must be taken whenever and wherever they can be found. The pain in Amy's family became the continuation and extension of her own experience of lovelessness. In this instance, the sins of the parent were placed upon the children. Amy's mother's lack of forgiveness left Amy so impoverished that she in turn could not give to her family what they deserved and needed.

Once one is in despair, though, where does that one turn for assistance? Amy was correct in seeking her pastor's help. The remedy offered to her draws on some psychologically sound and useful concepts. The Bible, too, offers some assistance in this matter.

A Word of Hope

The Emmaus story does not end with depression. Suddenly, by divine initiative, the risen Christ appeared to the disciples. The travelers' depression had been so heavy, they didn't even recognize the very one they hoped so much to see again. It appeared as though the disciples were wandering around, numbed by their shattered hopes, and unable to adequately see or interpret what was happening to them. Such is frequently the condition of individuals feeling overwhelmed by depression and despair. Jesus journeyed with them and questioned them. He tried to show them from the Bible why the events took place and what significance they held. The cross wasn't to be a crushing defeat but a resounding victory.

Evening drew near, and they shared a meal together. The disciples' eyes opened. Maybe it was the long journey, the chance to stretch their legs that finally woke them up. Maybe the hours of discussion, the chance to air their feelings and really be heard, unclogged their emotions. Maybe the reviewing of fond memories reignited their life fires. Maybe the good food or the Bible lesson did the trick. Surely the unconscious connection between this evening meal and previous meals with Jesus began to dawn on them. Perhaps some combination of all these possibilities opened their eyes.

All of these things can help us out of depression—exercise, talking it out, memories, adequate diet, the Bible. This encounter offered one more essential ingredient of personal healing. This one ingredient was the rekindled fire of hope within them. Somehow being with Christ also lifted them out of their despair. They had met the resurrected one, and they possessed again that essential zest for the remaining journeys of their lives.

They recognized their Companion, and the rest is gospel. Do you ever think about that? Had not the first few disciples been shaken out of their depression and despair, perhaps no one would have ever been able to adequately share the story of Jesus. If the travelers had continued throughout the rest of their journey with their faces and hearts filled with gloom, there might not be any adequate records of Christ's resurrection.

From the depths of despair, Jesus lifted their spirits to a redirected life. Beginning with a journey through Scripture, the gift of quality time, and a shared meal, Jesus Christ re-kindled the fires of life's hope within them. The two departed from their encounter with Jesus empowered again. Their imagination was alive again with the possibilities of a kingdom of God based in a hope of His loving, intimate presence with each of His children. An encounter with Christ reaffirmed their personhood and gave them the desire to go on.

Doesn't an encounter with Christ offer us the same thing? We know we have worth and our lives have purpose because we believe again that the whole Christ event was meaningful. God loves us so much that He chose to identify with us in our humanity in His Child, Jesus Christ. The Christ encounter links us again with our Maker and His purpose and destiny for us.

The human spirit needs opportunities for creative and imaginative hope. Imagination enables us to move beyond the sometimes limiting qualities of our current life situations. Imagination enables us to believe in a future with possibilities and to visualize the path we might take to make those possibilities into realities. Imagination is not just wishful thinking or an unrealistic denial of reality. The disciples on the road to Emmaus knew that Jesus had been killed violently. Closing their eyes and pretending that Calvary had not happened would have been an extreme form of denial, and it would not have served the Lord's intentions at all. Through their encounter with the risen Lord at Emmaus, they saw beyond the dark reality of the events of that week. The disciples regained their imaginative grasp on the larger picture of God's working in their lives and in the world around them. The regaining of that crucial imaginative hope of God's dynamic, forgiving action transformed their world and inspired their mission.

For Amy, her hope was centered around gaining her mother's forgiveness through years of attentive service to her mother. She lived those years with that single goal as the strongest force to give meaning in her existence. She sacrificed her relationship with her husband and had created an idol—a false god—in her vision of receiving her mother's blessing. When her mother died without absolving her of her guilt, Amy lost not only a relationship but the experience of having a center of meaning and purpose for her life.

Amy broke the Commandment to have no other gods before the Lord. Not till her mother's death did Amy realize how she steadily made her mother's blessing into an idol all those years. Eventually Amy's healing came with the combined help of both her psychiatrist and her pastoral counselor. The psychiatrist was able to stabilize the emotional components of her depression. The pastoral counselor was able to point her in the direction of a more dependable hope by helping her to gradually take back the power which she had given to her mother to determine her worthiness. Slowly Amy surrendered her lifelong compulsion to seek her mother's blessing and recognized her worth in the eyes of other people in her life. As acceptance and appreciation became more attainable through the ministry of her family and friends, she became aware of the potential for an experience of forgiveness and grace from God. She realized that her years of devotions and prayer were offered through the limited vessel of her mother. Amy discovered the freedom and release from guilt when she encountered the same risen Lord who had met the disciples on the road to Emmaus.

Herein lies an avenue for us to overcome the life-style of despair. Herein lies also the picture of the church. The church offers each of us these things: an encounter with Christ, solid grounding in Scripture, an offering of the gift of companionship, the sharing of a meal, and the revitalization of hope.

9

The Power-Seeking Life-Style

"He is so good! He has the arm of Roberto Clemente, the speed of Lou Brock, the power of Reggie Jackson, and he can hit for an average like Wade Boggs. He is the Tape Measure Kid, dare I say, the rebirth of Mickey Mantle or Willie Mays." It seems that every spring, baseball fans are bombarded with this type of media barrage about one young player or another. Each gifted player has it all, everything that anyone could want—money, popularity, or national exposure. All of these things are attributes of wealth and power.

Cliff was just like everyone else in his Sunday School class. New cars, bigger homes, stylish clothes, and expensive vacations seemed to be the substance of the pre-lesson conversation around the coffee pot each Sunday morning. Monday morning conversation with his work associates followed a similar vein but also expanded to include stock market ups and downs, investment potentials, and rising costs of college educations for his children. Cliff was caught in a life-style that doesn't appear to be self-defeating. In fact, Cliff's life-style seems to capture most of what the American work ethic and success myth teaches all of us.

Character Study: The Rich Ruler

Remember the biblical account of the rich ruler in Luke

18? That young man had a power-seeking problem too. Imagine with me that he was like one of today's gifted ball players: He had it all, the world by the string. His biggest worries were what he was going to buy and how many to get. He practically owned the town he lived in; only last week, they had decided to name a street after him. On one occasion, he stumbled upon a picnic. There among the trees and flowers were scores of people laughing, hugging, and eating. Everywhere were children playing. It seemed almost like a carnival was taking place.

The ruler's curiosity was up. "What's going on?" he kept asking people without getting a straight answer. Finally someone who seemed like a spokesman clued him in. Jesus told the ruler that this group was a gathering for God's kingdom. Everything he witnessed was just a part of kingdom living. Since it looked enjoyable, the ruler wanted to join in. Jesus agreed, and the ruler spent the better part of the day with Jesus and the disciples.

As the sun slowly set, Jesus invited the young ruler to join them. The ruler was eager to be with Jesus, but he had so many responsibilities with his monies that there was some question as to whether he could. Jesus said to him, "Go, sell all that you have, and distribute it to the poor, and you will gain the kingdom of God."

The ruler was sad because he was quite rich and he wanted to be with Jesus. He left, wishing there was some easier choice to make. The next morning took its time in coming. The young ruler tossed and turned all night. Finally, the sun peaked over the window sill. He had another chance! He raced to find Jesus.

When he got there, he found . . . nothing. He burst onto the lawn only to find three birds and a squirrel. Where

was the picnic? Where were the disciples and Jesus?
Where was the kingdom? Couldn't they wait? He made the
right choice; it just took time.

Jesus gives a shocking epilogue to the story. "How hard it
is for those who have riches to enter the kingdom of God!
For it is easier for a camel to go through the eye of a needle
than for a rich man to enter the kingdom." When asked by
the disciples, "Then it's impossible?" Jesus replied, "Without God, it is impossible."

Case Study: Cliff

Power is the currency in every human encounter, from
family relationships to international peace negotiations.
The idolatry of power doesn't become obvious to many of us
until, as with Cliff or the rich ruler, something intrudes and
reminds us of where our real concerns lie.

Cliff's seventeen-year-old son, Paul, ran away from home
and surfaced six months later in a commune several states
away. Paul's argument for abandoning the comforts of home
was a growing disillusionment with the hypocrisy of his parent's life-style in the face of both their espoused Christian
ideals and the realities of poverty in the world around them.

Paul's confrontation with Cliff is both true and naive. (It
also represents a common rebelliousness characteristic of
many adolescents toward their parent's life-styles which
may or may not have had anything to do with Cliff's eco-
nomic net worth.) Nevertheless, Cliff understood and felt
deeply the judgment of his son that echoed his own self-
awareness. He, like the rich ruler, was too invested in what
his riches symbolized in his own quest for power, prestige,
and social recognition.

To his credit, Cliff used the sharing context of a men's

retreat at church to struggle openly with the indictment of his son's rejection of his life-style. He found in the community of his own church that the concerns raised by his parent-child dilemma resonated with the secret conflicts in many of the hearts of his fellow church members. Together they began to explore openly the nature of their emotional and spiritual attachments to their possessions and their obsessions with the pursuit of power that so characterized their common concerns.

Analysis of the Power-Seeking Life-Style

The origin of the power-seeking life-style is less obvious than many of the other life-styles. It is also a life-style that gains considerable social and cultural approval in America. Raised in a country which values the great American dream as a possibility for any hardworking individual, Cliff is a caricature of the successful businessman or businesswoman. Like many churches, Cliff's church reinforces this dream with a curious kind of civil religion. Proponents of this type of religion preach God's blessing on successful American business while postponing concern about the injustice and poverty around the edges of this success. Cliff's son, Paul, like many children, has captured the paradox in this civil religion and personalized it with his father.

For decades, psychologists have assumed that excessive preoccupation with gaining power is an effort to compensate for deep-seated feelings of inferiority. Individuals who express this power-seeking life-style are persons for whom mere success is not enough personal satisfaction. Success is measured only in terms of how much superiority over one's peers or competitors is also achieved. This sense of inner inferiority is expressed through a form of anxiety which we experience as performance anxiety. Early in life, the power-seeking individual discovers that performance anxiety can be managed through a highly competitive response. The ability to monitor one's competitive drive and the effects that drive has on others is lost. Winning becomes the end that justifies the means. It is only a small step to jump from a preoccupation with winning at all costs to a preoccupation with winning by bigger and bigger margins. Later in life, the manner in which one wins is preoccupied with financial profits, income, management positions, advanced degrees, and the status symbols of expensive cars, homes, clothes, jewelry, and other "things." One's self-evaluation of worth becomes controlled by these external measurements of power and status. The insight that we are all equal in the eyes of God gets lost in the scramble to climb the power-success ladder.

The process of making power, money, and prestige into an idol is usually a slow procedure. Very few sensitive Christians would consciously set out to put their possessions and power-seeking efforts above their loyalty or commitment to God. The conversation around the coffee pot in Cliff's Sunday School is not meant to be sacrilegious or to replace their individual desire to study about God and His will for their lives. Until the inappropriateness of this behavior is pointed out by someone like the rebellious son, Paul, it goes unnoticed and seems to be very innocent.

A Word of Hope

Christ asked the rich young ruler to sell all his possessions and give the profits to the poor in order that he might be free to come follow Him. The concern for the lack of justice for the poor and the ways in which poverty can wear down one's sense of personal self-worth are obvious in Jesus's request to the rich young ruler. More importantly, the young ruler needed to rid himself of the external trappings of his success and power in order to be open to the deeper truths of life that Christ offered. When the ruler was captive to the symbols of his own self-worship, he could not understand the importance of self-surrender that was necessary to put the worship of God at the center of his life experience.

Much of the time, Christians concern themselves with the reality of the kingdom of God as a future event. In fact, there is considerable opportunity to interpret Christ's comments about the kingdom of God as a present reality within the individual lives of each believer. Interpreted in this manner, Christ's request of the rich ruler reflects His concern about the inner life of this man, as well as the outer manifestation of financial or political injustice. To experience the kingdom of God within himself, the rich ruler needed to give up his self-constructed standards of well-being and superiority and to see himself through the eyes of Christ: "Who, though he was in the form of God, did not count equality with God a thing to be grasped, but emptied himself, taking the form of a servant" (Phil. 2:6). This kind of radical reinterpretation of one's values and self-worth was immediately impossible for the rich young ruler, and he left his encounter with Jesus very saddened, knowing that he could not release himself from his power-seeking life-style that simply.

Cliff's journey out of his self-defeating life-style was encouraged by the continuing support of the men's prayer group at church and his desire to redeem his relationship to Paul. The outward manifestations of his power-seeking life-style had not progressed to the same degree as the rich young ruler in the biblical story. Cliff had not yet completed the climb to the top of the power ladder, and he was able to apply his knowledge of the Christian faith to help him make a mid-course correction.

To overcome this self-defeating life-style, Cliff made some recommitments. He closely examined the underlying motivations for his need to achieve power. Identifying his lingering inferiority feelings from earlier in life, he reinterpreted their meaning in light of his current, more mature perspective. Finally, with a rededication of his life to the higher calling of Christ Jesus, Cliff reorganized his priorities without sacrifice to his profession or his family.

10

The Entertainer Life-Style

The entertainer is one who needs attention or affection and uses his imagination or creativity to draw individuals to himself through entertainment. The instrument of entertainment may be song, dance, athletic ability, sleight of hand, or humor. The key is that regardless of the instrument, the entertainer is trying to purchase someone's attention with the instrument. If the audience enjoys the performance, the entertainer has bought what he wanted.

Character Study: Simon

The Bible contains some examples of persons who had an entertainer life-style. Simon the Great of Acts 8:9-25 is a good example. Simon was a Samaritan who practiced magic. This magic might have been sleight of hand or full-fledged occult practices; we don't really know. What we do know is that the Bible records that he was quite good at his craft. All of the people were amazed at his magic. As Simon proclaimed himself as somebody great, the people echoed that a great power of God was with him. It was beautiful, just what Simon wanted. The people loved him. All the years of seeking admiration had finally paid off when Simon went public with his traveling magic show.

Simon was not the only crowd-drawing phenomenon in Samaria. Philip the disciple was in Samaria as well, and he was drawing his share of crowds. There was a difference, though. When Simon performed, the people were amazed. When Philip preached the gospel of Christ, the people believed and were baptized. Even Simon, after he heard Philip, believed, was baptized, and traveled with Philip. As Simon stayed with Philip, he witnessed many signs and miracles that amazed him.

So much was happening in Samaria that the church in Jerusalem sent Peter and John there to see what needed to be done. When Peter and John arrived, they laid hands on the new converts so that they might receive the Holy Spirit. Simon became envious of this new thing. He had tried magic, and that had worked to some extent. He had become a Christian, and that gave him some of the attention he craved. Now there was this laying on of hands and the connection with the Holy Spirit. Simon knew within himself that this was the ultimate achievement. He would have arrived finally, and he would be accepted.

So Simon offered to buy the process of laying on of hands. We can almost hear his offer, "Peter, I have checked the market value, and I believe I can offer you a good price. I would like to buy the Laying on of Hands/Indwelling of the Holy Spirit procedure for ten thousand dollars." The boldness of many modern translations cannot go ignored on Peter's response, "May you and your money go to hell!" (Acts 8:20, GNB). Shocking words, yes, but no less shocking than Simon's offer, and no less true than Simon's tragic condition. Simon's life-style was leading him on a road to destruction, a road to hell.

Case Study: Daryl

Most of us are more familiar with another type of

entertainer—the clown. People love to laugh and are drawn to a clown. Look at any party, the one making people laugh is where the crowd is. Take children to a circus, and outside of the animals, they will remember the clowns.

Daryl was noted throughout the county for his sense of humor and the fact that he always kept a current set of jokes to tell his customers and his many friends who dropped by his auto shop during the week. Within his circles in town, he and his wife consistently were invited to parties and socials because of his quick wit and outgoing personality. Any social event would start smoothly if Daryl attended.

Three years ago Daryl's elementary-age and youngest child, Cory, was involved in a serious hit-and-run automobile accident and was hospitalized for four months. The first six weeks of this hospitalization, Cory laid comatose in the intensive care unit at the state medical college in the capital city thirty-five miles away. The doctors literally did not know through those weeks whether Cory would ever regain consciousness and survive her hospitalization. Finally, after five serious operations, the pressure on the spinal column was relieved, which reduced the pressure internally in Cory's brain. She became responsive to external stimuli and regained consciousness.

Daryl had a limited insurance policy which was inadequate to cover the medical expenses for Cory's hospitalization. Several churches and civic groups in the community held emergency fund-raising drives and gave blood on Cory's behalf. Despite these efforts, Daryl still had to go to the bank to borrow several hundred thousand dollars against the future assets of his business in order to cover the hospital bills.

Throughout this ordeal, as in other experiences in his life,

Daryl continued to be the funny man. He tried to lift people's spirits who came to the hospital or to his home to give him and his wife support. He constantly decorated Cory's hospital room with posters and balloons. He pulled gags and pranks on the hospital nurses and personnel with whom he and his wife became close during Cory's hospitalization. Everyone in the community and in the hospital was amazed at the nature of Daryl's coping mechanisms except his wife, Bonny. She knew he was just putting on a show to cover his deep and profound fear and agony. Finally she persuaded Daryl to accept an offer from the hospital chaplain to drop by and talk about his experience.

The chaplain soon discovered what he had suspected all along. Daryl actually was depressed and frightened. He shared with the chaplain that fear and depression had been with him for many years before the accident. Daryl described how throughout his adolescence he always had been smaller than other boys his age and somewhat uncoordinated. Very early in life, Daryl discovered that he could make people laugh. By being cute, he could turn potentially threatening situations around toward his favor. He reported with some pride how on several occasions, like other boys his age, he had managed to get in trouble at school or home or church. He postponed any serious punishment for deeds by making his parents, teacher, or other authority figure laugh at him. Whenever his grades were questionable, his sense of humor produced a benefit-of-a-doubt response from his teachers with a higher grade than he really deserved. On at least one occasion, he persuaded a bully to leave him alone by launching into a series of jokes that completely disarmed his adversary's anger.

Daryl lamented that he didn't know how to be with people except to be the class clown. He did not see himself as an attractive person or intelligent enough in academics to compete with his peers. He relied on jokes or practical gags to get the attention and affection that he desperately needed. He also suspected that people were so accustomed to seeing him as a funnyman that they didn't know how to respond to the other emotions he carried within himself. The crisis with Cory, however, caused some of Daryl's inner fear and sadness to leak out around the edges of his personality and confirmed his suspicions. Even his closest friends had difficulty hearing the expression of his sad feelings. They responded in a way which communicated clearly to Daryl that they wanted to see his comical side again. Daryl wanted to let others see the full range of his emotions, but he didn't know how to begin.

Analysis of the Entertainer Life-Style

Daryl's story is familiar because we are all aware of how humor is used to hide one's real emotions. We use humor to avoid feeling anger, shame, guilt, and sadness. We reinforce others' efforts to hide their pain through humor when we so easily join them in their hollow laughter. We also understand the symbolic role that clowns have always played in the circus. The clown is a distractor of the crowd's attention during tense moments in the circus act. The rodeo clown races in to the center ring to draw the attention of the fierce raging bull in the rodeo, protecting the fallen cowboy from a sudden trampling of the out-of-control beast. And the clown in the puppet shows is able to help us cry and laugh at the same time as he portrays in comical fashion our common human frailties.

Clowning, entertaining, and laughter are common human experiences across time and culture. There are mentions of the entertaining life-style in the Bible. Laughter, for example, is mentioned in both Testaments. The biblical understanding of laughter, though, is different than what we might expect. For us, laughter means happy times, carefree moments as one might have enjoying playful puppies or even the comical twists we find in the midst of our daily routines. Laughter is spontaneous and releases our emotions in a positive experience of shared joy. For the ancient mind, laughter communicated a much more serious and negative tone. Those who laughed were those who were in a superior role in life. They made fun of and toyed with the common people. They enjoyed poking fun at those who were their "inferiors." The Beatitudes of Luke 6 condemn those who laugh. Sometimes, God was described as one who laughed, as in Psalm 59:8, as though He were playing some grand joke on the people.

The biblical understanding of laughter is helpful to our understanding of the entertainer life-style and the plight of Daryl. We are reminded that sometimes the entertainer is covering fear and anxieties by using humor as a defense to gain acceptance. Without this defense, the entertainer fears rejection or perhaps the worse fate of being totally unnoticed by others. Ironically, the very individual whom the entertainer courts, the entertainer fears. While the entertainer seeks to rise above others, he or she actually feels inferior to them.

Another biblical use of the entertainer concept communicates an awareness of qualities normally attributed to children. In Proverbs 26:19 and Isaiah 3:16-18, the idea of clowning is expressed by a term which literally means "to act like a child." In fact, the Isaiah reference specifically refers to little cymbals attached to the ankles of little girls. Again, we find a useful biblical understanding for our purposes. In some instances, those who hide within the entertainer life-style are seeking to live within the safety of childlike play, amusing themselves without facing the adult world of responsibilities.

Contemporary psychology has established that the capacity to approach life with the playful imagination of the child is crucial to our ability to face life with an attitude of hopefulness. Children have to learn how to respond to life's challenges with fear. Children are not restricted in their responses like adults, who have lost the capacity to approach that which they fear with the playful capacity to use imagination to overcome their fears. The entertainer, who approaches life and its accompanying anxieties with the same strategies of the child, has lost the crucial facility of reality testing in combination with a playfulness about the contents of that same reality.

Poets and playwrights have struggled with this need we all have for comic relief of the pain and stresses of life. Songwriters have focused on the clown image effectively. Several years ago, a popular song by Smokey Robinson and the Miracles was "The Tears of a Clown." The song describes the agony of a broken relationship and uses the image of a clown crying quietly alone as the only description of his feelings. The clown cries alone to hide the grief and the hopelessness that is felt in this experience. Any other hurts and problems which are felt to be unexpressible but can be handled with the humorous denial of the clown could have been substituted.

Daryl felt trapped by a lifelong strategy of hiding his true feelings and fears behind the socially acceptable facade of the playful, funny young man. An early effort to compensate for the feelings of inadequacy and insecurity that he experienced as a young boy had become a lifelong means of defining himself in all relationships. The significant friendships he relied on were limited by his lack of experience in sharing his real feelings of anxiety and inadequacy.

Now faced with the serious and life-threatening illness of Cory, Daryl continued to take care of others' anxieties as well as his own by wearing the familiar mask of the clown. The tragedy is not just Daryl's, however. His friends were losing out on several uniquely human opportunities to share his burdens and to experience the mutually important gift of love. They joined his resistance to letting his real and vulnerable self become available. The opportunity for their friendship to be deepened in that sharing was forever lost.

A Word of Hope

Some of the most precious moments we can experience occur when we are able to enter into another person's anguish. In so doing, we experience the fullness of the scriptural injunction of Galatians 6:2 to "bear one another's burdens, and so fulfil the law of Christ."

As in many other life-style strategies, the strategy of the entertainer reflects a potentially constructive and hopeful approach to life. The consistent and indiscriminate usage produces a life-style that distorts reality. Whether the motives of the modern-day entertainer reflect the efforts to hide one's anxieties in the laughter of false superiority or reflect an effort to hide behind the innocent memories of childhood, the entertainer takes the potentially useful response to anxiety of humor and distorts it.

The entertainer is hiding behind a shield of entertainment. The shield protects him from the fear of being recognized and rejected. Though the shield may bring enjoyment to audiences, it only serves to teach the entertainer that he is valuable only for the entertainment he provides. This results in a personality hell. The individual believes that he must earn constantly and be more creative and entertaining at each turn of the road. It is a road that both Simon and Daryl chose in our stories. It is a road running diametrically with the path of grace displayed to each of us in the presence of Jesus Christ. In Christ, we find the acceptance we need to give us the power to overcome this life-style.

11

The Dreamer Life-Style

Case Study: Sharon

Sharon loved to daydream. Doesn't everyone? She could get lost in her dream world for hours at a time. Even as a college junior, she still spent a large amount of time in her dreams. When her friends began making fun of her and accusing her of unrealistic thoughts, Sharon went to her campus minister for counseling.

Sharon believed her friends were referring to her tendency to tune out thoughts which created conflict for her and replace them with thoughts that made her happy. Sharon described a very effective way of withdrawing from her classes and retreating to a very rich and colorful fantasy world of her daydreams. She developed this talent for tuning out external distractions and used it as a survival technique in her childhood at an orphanage. Sharon recalled experiences in the orphanage when eight or ten children were involved in playing, and she retreated quietly into her daydream, totally oblivious of her surroundings. She also reported that her powers of concentration were so great that, if she needed to, she could focus on her studies and lose track of everything for up to eight or ten hours at a time. Sharon had a straight A average but did not have any significant close relationships, even with her girl friends in the dorm.

What was upsetting Sharon was that those whose acceptance she wanted the most were giving her the most consistent critical feedback. One young man in her chemistry lab had been showing considerable interest in Sharon for several weeks. She believed that he enjoyed her sense of humor and found her to be an interesting conversationalist. She was crushed when a girl friend told her that this young man thought that she was a very "spacey" person. This same girl friend was the one who urged Sharon to seek help with her dreamer life-style.

The campus minister noticed how difficult it was for Sharon to stay tuned to the painful issues that were raised in her counseling. He was aware that she moved in and out emotionally and interjected inappropriate comments to the subjects they were discussing. If he tried to trace her thought pattern in any particular discussion, she drifted away, forgetting large segments of the session. When he challenged this response, Sharon became agitated and protested the topic of evaluation.

Sometimes Sharon began sessions by telling the minister very elaborate stories which he assumed were true until midway through the story he realized she was describing one of her dream states or fantasies. Sharon, though, would be surprised by his confusing reality and her imagination when it was very clear to her which was which. Sharon agreed with him, however, that it would be useful to discern when people were having difficulty understanding from her what was real and what was imaginary.

Several weeks into their counseling, Sharon began to describe very painful nightmares containing a lot of violence which she did not understand. It frightened her to have her sleep disrupted in this way, especially since she was not aware of feeling angry or aggressive toward anyone that she knew.

The dream world is a confusing and misunderstood realm. Often, dreams are simply a mixture of events and images from the previous day. At other times, though, dreams are a link with strong unconscious feelings which the conscious is ignoring. The unconscious uses dreams as an outlet to communicate these strong feelings. The feelings may relate to actual fact or to perceived fact. In either case, the unconscious treats the two with the same intensity. This is to say, the individual may be equally troubled by dreams which deal with a real crisis or an imagined crisis.

Character Study: Joseph

In the Bible, we learn of a dreamer: Joseph. Genesis 37 records the story of Joseph and his dreamer life-style. We generally remember the story because of Joseph's coat of many colors. The coat was just one of many gifts that showed that Joseph was Jacob's favorite son. If you know any favorite children, you know how intolerable they can be. It seems that they can get away with anything, and they seem to get everything. What is really irritating about favorites is not the abundance of gifts that are showered upon them but their sense of entitlement for those gifts. The presence of gratitude is lost with a favorite child.

Joseph was an extreme example of a favorite child. He was the child of his father's favorite wife. Though not the youngest, he was one of the youngest. He was a child in his father's old age, a last chance at youth. So Joseph received his share of gifts. On a well-known occasion, he received a lavish gift, a coat of many pretty colors, while his brothers received nothing. The tendency of favorite children is to make demands on others and assume that his or her way is the only way. I can imagine that Joseph lived up to this tendency with his brothers.

Ironically, that wasn't what upset Joseph's brothers. They could tolerate all of Joseph's antics—everything except his dreams. If you remember, Joseph had a lively dream life. We don't know if Joseph had normal dreams like you or I. Most of us dream of getting rich or having the ability to fly or something else in that vein. Joseph had even bigger dreams.

For instance, one day Joseph called all eleven brothers together to tell them about a dream. It seems that Joseph and his brothers were out in the field binding together bundles of wheat. Suddenly Joseph's bundle stood upright and rose above everyone else's. The remaining bundles all bowed down to Joseph's bundle. You can imagine how displeased Joseph's brothers were with the obvious implications of that dream.

The next day Joseph told them another dream. In this one, the sun, moon, and stars bowed down to Joseph. This might have been the last straw, for shortly thereafter, Joseph's brothers began plotting a way to get rid of Joseph.

The original plan was to kill Joseph. An alternative was chosen, though, and Joseph was shipped off to Egypt. I guess they figured they would be safe from his annoying dreams with Joseph in Egypt. After some time, Joseph gained some prominence in Egypt as a dream interpreter. Talk about events coming about full circle, now Joseph was in the official business of explaining the pharaoh's dreams. In time, all of Joseph's dreams came true. Joseph's brothers came to Egypt and were in Joseph's debt. It seems that Joseph's dreams were an avenue of communication into matters that everyone's conscious mind was unaware of. That is to say, Joseph's dreams related truths that were hidden to the conscious mind.

Analysis of the Dreamer Life-Style

Both Joseph and Sharon had some annoying qualities to their life-style. They both managed to alienate other people in the process of expressing their hopes, needs, and fears in their dreaming way. Neither of them realized that their withdrawal into their inner world would result in the level of rejection by other people along the way. Neither were they aware of how much pride was a part of their personalities. The more they withdrew from the real world into the private world of their dreams, the more prideful each became.

Dreams can be very alluring and powerful. The presence of unconscious truths disguised in dream pictures acts on the consciousness of the dreamer. The dreamer becomes distracted from the normal day-to-day concerns of life. The already natural distractedness of dreaming compounds the willful decision to retreat into dreams.

Sharon's story is an excellent example of the usefulness of the dreamer life-style as a way of coping with anxiety-producing incidents. Sharon grew up in an orphanage, an environment which was very chaotic and unpredictable. With no durable relationships available, Sharon learned how to rely on her own coping skills. She possessed an exceptional mind with the capacity to concentrate on one subject and block out everything else from her awareness. She discovered in the orphanage how useful this skill was, and she refined her ability to mentally and emotionally remove herself from the chaos around her by concentrating on something less stressful and more appealing to her. This remarkable strategy saved her from being overwhelmed by the stresses and anxieties in her environment.

Unfortunately for Sharon, her strategy not only saved her from excessive anxiety but also isolated her from all relationships. She was socially inept and unaware of how her behavior affected others adversely. The earliest sign of anxiety triggered an automatic response of withdrawal into her daydreaming state, and she inevitably merged real experience with imaginary fantasy. This process was so complete that Sharon didn't realize that other people could not decipher her conversation. No one could tell how much was reality and what was her own unique interpretations, unless someone pointed this out to her.

Joseph's development of the dreamer life-style emerged out of a different set of life circumstances than Sharon's. Where Sharon grew up an abandoned child living in a state-funded orphanage, Joseph grew up in a large family in the privileged position of favorite child. Though the favorite child enjoys certain advantages over the rest of the children in the family, he frequently experiences anxiety and fears of losing the favored position. He also lives with an awareness of how his status in the family fosters resentment in the other children, and he may grow up feeling guilt and resentment for having been "set apart." The position of being the "special child" was thrust upon Joseph by his father, though the consequences produced the same kind of alienation that Sharon's self-imposed isolation gave to her. Both Sharon and Joseph lacked the social skills and interpersonal effectiveness to engage others in healthy interaction. "Special children" grow up believing that others will always treat them as unique and will frequently set up rejection by others in their expectation that they will be granted undue considerations.

A Word of Hope

Overcoming the self-defeating aspects of the dreamer life-style involves a slow and painful process of learning to face anxiety without the luxury of retreating into daydreams. As Sharon was encouraged to resist this temptation to retreat, she became more and more distraught. Her dreams revealed an underlying rage that needed to be understood. Sharon had trouble seeing both an angry interior and a happy exterior to her personality. She discovered that an entire part of her personality which she saw as angry, unhappy, and hurt had been hidden within her, almost forgotten. As she explored this hurt, frightened little girl within her, she began to show the capacity to tolerate anxiety more maturely. Sharon's relationships grew more mutually satisfying because she was able to persevere in the face of anxiety at those moments where she might have chosen to retreat in the past. The quality of her communication became more realistic and less "spacey." She discovered that other people were genuinely interested in her.

Joseph was not able to persist in the charade of being lord over his father and brothers. The pain of the separation and the desire to experience brotherly closeness quickly overrode Joseph's need for revenge and his desire to have his brothers treat him as "special" anymore. The restoration of Joseph's relationships with his brothers required him to surrender the "favorite child" role and to meet his brothers as equals. To be an equal with another person requires surrendering the illusions we have about ourselves as "above the world," and it requires that we explore our similarities with the rest of humanity.

Spiritually, the challenge of surrendering the false pride of being "special" is also very difficult. If letting go of the illusion of being the "favorite child" of his earthly father was difficult, it was even more challenging for Joseph to let go of the image of being king over all humanity. Ironically, in the case of Joseph and Sharon, when the illusion of being special was surrendered, the experience of equality with others was very freeing. No longer did they live with the secret dread of failure or of being discovered as counterfeit. No longer was the prospect of falling from the position of "favorite child" to be feared and defended against. Fear was replaced with love and acceptance. Each encountered a greater sense of community and communion than had ever been imagined.

12

The Workaholic Life-Style

Case Study: The Reverend Mr. John Jaspers

John Jaspers has been the successful pastor of the Old First Church for fifteen years. Successful, yes, but at quite a price. Imagine a full work week for church responsibilities, serving on the administrative boards of three community service agencies, being president of the local ministerial association, and being a trustee at the local college. Jaspers must be working sixty or more hours a week. When asked about his perspectives on his life and work, he confessed that though he was overcommitted he did not feel he was doing enough. His fear was that he still might not be noticed by his peers to ever be considered for his dream to teach at the college.

What a tragic picture of human existence! Working day in and day out to gain recognition or approval and, sadly, not giving oneself the credit to find one's life goals attainable, John Jaspers is battling with the workaholic life-style.

A workaholic is one who works compulsively and fits the biblical picture found in Luke 10:38-42. There, the image is of one who acts because that is compelled, pressured, in distress, or it is a necessity. The image is a situation of need where one is compelled to act because no other option was perceived. The Hebrew counterpart to this concept implies narrowness or constraint. How often is the Christian faith portrayed as undesirable because it is too constraining? In contrast, the actual case is that the Christian faith opens up the freedom to be whole and the wide range to be oneself. A workaholic is one who chooses the narrow option to be lost in work, to define oneself by one's achievement of work responsibilities. This choice is perceived to be easiest because the other ever-changing choices are too frightening.

The physical results from this type of behavior fall short of what human existence can be. John Jaspers has been burning his candle at both ends for fifteen years. He has aches and pains in every system of his body. At his last physical exam, the doctor noted high blood pressure, migraine headaches, and chronic, low back pain. Coupled with the physical ailments, John suffers emotionally as well. His normal emotional level seems to be at depression, and he honestly could not tell you which of his many commitments could be cut back. He is being scheduled by his own fears and commitments, and it is killing his existence.

The case of John Jaspers reminds us of ourselves at times. We, too, can fall into a life-style of letting our schedule run our lives. We are afraid, and we can't deal with those fears. We become like Martha in the New Testament. She definitely displayed a workaholic life-style to deal with her fears. Some people eat compulsively, others watch TV, still others work—work like there is no tomorrow, work to lose themselves in the effort, work to avoid something they are afraid to face—a family, bills, old age, death, you name it.

Character Study: Mary and Martha

In the Mary and Martha story of Luke 10, Mary and Martha prepared for a special house guest. Martha insisted that everything be just right. The house had to be in order, the bath tub had to be scrubbed, the big family Bible had to be on the coffee table (opened to the twenty-third Psalm, of course), and the most sumptuous feast had to be concocted. When Jesus arrived, Martha was still hustling about, barely wiping her hands on her apron to shake His, then she was off to the kitchen again. Mary on the other hand, sat down at Jesus' feet and played the candid host.

Martha became quite upset. This was a very important time—a special guest, a special house arrangement, and a special meal. Some evaluation of her would be based on all these things. Things must be at their best, or folk would think less of Martha. Martha's anxiety built until she finally stormed into Jesus' presence and asked for Mary's chastisement (or her own endorsement). She expected Jesus to applaud her and reprimand Mary. All of her life, it had been this way. Martha did all the work; Mary sat around and batted her eyes at the boys. Surely this time Martha would be proved right.

The most surprising thing happened, though. Jesus apparently had something different in mind for this drama. Instead of reprimanding Mary, Jesus chastised Martha. Jesus said, "Martha, you feel you must do so many things, and, therefore, many things trouble you. There is only one thing that has this 'must do' aspect about it. Mary has chosen the good part."

Analysis of the Workaholic Life-Style

Unfortunately workaholics think they are choosing the good part. Workaholism is a common self-destructive life-style for ministers and other helping professionals. The added expectations of the clergy to fulfill the New Testament model of servanthood increases the risk for a life-style of workaholism. Within this role of servant, it is difficult for a clergy person to say no to any request for ministry or service. Every request for help becomes an opportunity to fulfill the maximum of Jesus' statements the "first shall be last; and the last shall be first" (Matt. 19:30, KJV) or minister unto "the least of these" (Matt. 25:40). When the individual ego's need for affirmation is added to these internal "spiritual mandates," the workaholic life-style becomes easy.

Grandiosity is the secret sin of the workaholic. John Jaspers believes that no task is performed adequately unless undertaken by himself. For him and other clergy, this grandiose sense of pride is disguised under the idealism of servanthood or of "winning the lost to Jesus" by following in His path. For all workaholics, however, the grandiosity and prideful efforts to be superresponsible for every commitment undermines their efforts to be accepted for themselves. The curse of the workaholic life-style is that each success becomes the standard for all future efforts. Every success must be matched or bettered in order to maintain the myth of their responsibility.

Jesus made some perplexing statements to Martha about responsibility. There is much discussion as to what Jesus was referring to in His words to Martha. For us, it seems that Jesus was saying there is really only one thing to do or be anxious about. There is only one thing to be confined by, one narrow way to follow. The one thing is to let go and truly be yourself. Put away fears or anxieties of what you think people expect from you. Just be yourself.

Jesus confronted Martha's excessive workaholism as an excuse to avoid her primary task of celebrating the freedom of personhood in the opportunities or relationship with Him. We are reminded of the popular expression, "All work and no play makes Jack a dull boy." The simple truth is that even Christ sought an occasional retreat from the demands of His work and the intense emotional and physical drains of the pressing mass of people who followed Him. In Luke 4:42, Jesus went far enough away from the rest that the disciples searched for Him. The workaholic, though, is unable to follow the example of Christ, who occasionally passed over opportunities to minister to the needs of others to minister to His own needs for rest, relaxation, and renewal. The workaholic ignores references like Matthew 8:18, where Jesus left the crowd for a boat ride on the Sea of Galilee. For the workaholic, the anxiety of being human and limited, or of feeling insignificant and commonplace, drives him or her to a compulsive need for work. For them, only excellence in work can postpone the pain of that anxiety.

As in the other self-defeating life-styles, the workaholic style is a distortion of the innately creative effort to cope with the anxiety of our finiteness. Work is therapeutic for a healthy personality, and it is in keeping with God's intention for a full and productive life. Individuals work to stretch their abilities and to maximize their potential strengths. Work can stimulate emotional and spiritual growth as it helps the individual find achievement past what might have been expected. The workaholic, however, has lost touch with how important play and rest are to bring balance to the intensity of one's work and vocation.

A Word of Hope

Remember the conclusion to the Martha story was to relax and be one's self. How can you be yourself? Strive to be yourself as you strive to follow Jesus. Look at the context of this story in Luke 10. Jesus visited Mary and Martha immediately following the parable of the good Samaritan. As the Samaritan overcame his fears and anxieties to care for the wounded man, so Martha needed to overcome hers. The Samaritan was not bound by fear but free to care. Jesus was saying the same thing to Martha. Do not be bound by anything other than who you are in your relationship to Christ. Seize the moment for itself to be yourself. Explore your potential without being confined by your shortcomings. Let go of fear, and grab hold of Christ.

Pastor John Jaspers must return to his first commitment to God to overcome his workaholic life-style. The first commitment to God is an acceptance of the finitude of being human. Only by God's infinite grace and power can human beings find the strength to cope with the stress and pressures of life. John needs to allow God to be God again. The baptismal affirmation, "Jesus is Lord," includes Jesus' lordship over our souls *and* our work. Someone else can occasionally do what needs to be done. In most situations, even if the helper completely fails the task, the situation is not hopeless. There is time to correct most mistakes. The doctor's advice to Pastor Jaspers was to slow down, let associates or active laypersons shoulder some of the load. The doctor ordered him to schedule specific weekly time for recreation, be it sports, reading, family time, or the arts.

Mary chose the good part. The good part is relaxing. The good part includes visiting with friends, sharing thoughts and fears, and enjoying a good meal. That does sound good, doesn't it? Wouldn't life be more enjoyable if we all slowed down just a fraction? Maybe we, like Martha, should choose likewise (lifewise?).

Conclusion
Biblical and Psychological
Understanding of Personhood

There are a variety of ways to experience a self-defeating life-style. We have seen in each chapter a specific life-style strategy in combination with both biblical character studies and contemporary case studies. The ageless quality of these self-defeating patterns has been revealed, as well as the tendency to use these strategies throughout human history.

Biblical Principles

Several key principles are attested to in both Holy Scripture and in the modern human behavioral sciences that describe the nature of creative personhood. The first principle is that individuals are created to grow and develop. God did not intend for humans to be fixed or unchanging. Rather, Genesis 1:28 records that God commanded Adam to go out, grow, and multiply.

Each life story contains critical incidents and relationships that play a major role in the development of personality styles. The characters in the Bible all are described as persons on a life journey. Each of them interacted with others and with God. The interactions carry important elements in their developing understanding about themselves and their spiritual goals and needs. A portion of each incident is drawn from the story and internalized within an individual. These portions carry future significance and meaning in the developing self-understanding. Their life stories are the narratives of their interactions with family, friends, and enemies. The presence of God was acknowledged directly in inexplainable encounters with His Holy Spirit or indirectly through the testimony and influence of other people.

The second principle is that humans need relationships. God created man and woman to be in community, as noted in Genesis 2:18. Regardless of the role that a person eventually played in the course of biblical history, each reflected the basic human desire to be in relationship to others. This requirement of individuals to be in relationship in order to feel fulfillment is part of our nature as "in the image of God" (1:27). The biblical witness seems to point to this same quality within God. The desire for company and fulfillment in relationships could be behind all the divine activity from creation to redemption. We do not presume to know the mind and will of God, but it appears from reading the Bible that maintaining a quality of relationship with humankind has been, and continues to be, at the center of God's activities. It is plausible, then, that the desire for relationships is natural in creative personhood.

The third principle is that through the entrance of sin into an individual's life, each person experiences himself or herself as broken, inadequate, morally bankrupt, and ultimately unwhole. Adam's recognition of nakedness in Genesis 3:7 is indicative of this experience. Each biblical person struggled to find solutions to the feelings of personal inadequacy and unfulfillment by using self-centered strategies and various idolatrous endeavors. Eventually the truth of one's estrangement (sinfulness) was embraced. Finally, the idols were cast aside for genuine dependence upon the grace of God to render the experience of wholeness that was longed for. This change of direction and desire is what we interpret as conversion, and it is similar in its final consequences in both Old Testament and New Testament stories. Of course, the New Testament importance of an encounter with the living Christ is understood as the ultimate revelation about the potential for the healing of our personhood.

The encounter with Christ is understood throughout this book as the primary vehicle through which a self-defeating life-style is overcome and a more effective state of personal balance is achieved. The importance of this experience of grace is understood as the final and only long-term solution to the problem of human anxiety. Anxiety is the common enemy at the root of each of the life-style strategies explored in this book. Anxiety is both natural and inevitable to the human condition after the fall of humankind and the entrance of sin and alienation into our experience.

The Role of Anxiety in Human Experience

The previous chapters introduced the relationship of pride, shame, guilt, despair, dependence, sexual seductiveness, hostility, manipulation, controlling others, passivity, power seeking, apathy, workaholism, and even humor/entertainment to this core issue of anxiety. To be sure, it must be stated again that the interconnection between these life-style strategies and the experience of anxiety is complex and unique in the life story of each individual. The importance of the significant life experiences, the influence of family and friends, and the age and maturity of the individual all are factors. The blending of these factors determines the receptiveness to the ultimate experience of grace as the balancing force to overcome a self-defeating life-style. The importance of a pastoral counseling perspective has been encouraged as one relationship where the psychological, relational, and spiritual issues can be understood in preparing the way for the moment of grace that interrupts the self-defeating patterns.

The testimony of modern psychology underscores many of these ageless biblical principles as well. The crucible of the human personality is the family. Within the earliest significant relationships with mother, father, and siblings, the child first develops the core of its personality. Many psychologists believe that the essential structure and dynamics of the personality is in place by the time the child enters grammar school. This is not to say that changes cannot occur after this age or that the child has no capacity to alter his or her life patterns under the influence of other significant relationships and experiences. Change can and does occur, though usually under extenuating circumstances of life. A major shift in the living environment, extensive counseling, or a radical life-changing crisis situation can alter one's personality.

What is believed to be true is that the basic ingredients of healthy or unhealthy personality structures are fixed through interactions with family, siblings, and baby-sitters by the time of entering school. After that point of development, most individuals are in the process of putting meat on the bones of the skeleton of the personality.

This understanding of human personality development places a heavy responsibility upon the parents and other parental figures in the child's emotional development. Self-defeating life-style patterns are extensions of what is learned during this stage of personality development. These patterns are transmitted through example from parent to child, baby-sitter to child, or teacher to child. The intensity and importance of the relationship to the child is a significant variable in determining how deeply the child incorporates this example within his or her own life strategies.

The relationship between the personality of the child and the life-style strategies is somewhat complex. We have used the term *life-style strategies* to differentiate between personality structure and the accompanying patterned behavioral responses to anxiety. Authority figures in a child's early experience influence both the basic personality structure and these accompanying life-style strategies. Patterned behavioral responses to anxiety are controlled more consciously than personality traits. So they can be changed more easily than can the basic structure of the personality itself. Both personality structure and the accompanying emotional and behavioral patterns are internalized within the child. Life-style patterns continue to evolve throughout the life cycle of the maturing individual.

The previous chapters gave examples of some of the ways in which this process of internalization of a life-style occurs. Again, we say that the examples given are just examples; they are not offered as the final word on how the process occurs in every unique individual. Likewise, the solutions to the problems in each life-style strategy that have been illustrated are only illustrations of how the life-styles can be modified to find more effectiveness in living. Each person must find his own pathway and allow for the unpredictable impact of God's grace in this process.

The Relationship of Forgiveness to Anxiety

The resolution of each self-defeating life-style involved a

confrontation of the excessive and self-defeating qualities of the life-style, an exploration of the meaning and the development of the strategy, and an effort to change the strategy to offer a more balanced response to anxiety. The patterns of self-defeating attitudes and behaviors have also revealed an imbalance in the spiritual perspective of the individuals as well. We concede that many of the elements of the self-defeating patterns can be evaluated and changed successfully without an exploration of the spiritual dimensions of the person's experience. However, we believe that the most effective life-style changes occur when the spiritual implications of the life-style are also engaged and modified.

Since we have found that anxiety is the inevitable state for humanity which is estranged from God, we conclude that anxiety has both a spiritual origin and a necessary spiritual resolution. Throughout the Scriptures, the solution to humankind's estranged state of sin involves a confrontation of the sin and estrangement, followed by repentance within the welcome of God's grace. Forgiveness and acceptance are therefore the solutions to the problem of anxiety and self-defeating life-styles.

Forgiveness in each case study in the preceding chapters was imparted through relationships with family, friends, church, and pastoral counselor. Forgiveness involves an experience of feeling loved and accepted in spite of one's incompleteness, inadequacies, and failings. For forgiveness to be complete, the individual is enabled to forgive himself or herself through the recognition that in Christ God has also forgiven the individual and no further judgment is needed. When the individual realizes that to be worthy enough in God's eyes means to be worthy enough in his or her own eyes, then that individual is ready to accept forgiveness.

At the heart of the experience of forgiveness is the activation of love as the power to negate the anxiety that is felt. By love, we are referring to the experience of love as *agape* in the New Testament. *Agape* is love offered for no purpose except the enhancement of the worth of the loved one. It is an expression of goodwill that sees through the confused and self-destructive consequences of anxiety and attempts to behold the other person through the eyes of Christ, who has already loved him or her.

The ability to see other persons in their brokenness, confusion, and self-destructive life-styles requires an extraordinary capacity to transcend one's own limitations and fears as well. It is impossible to respond in this manner unless one has experienced forgiveness and the cancellation of one's own anxieties and limitations. The power of this need for the experience of forgiveness is at the heart of the parable of the prodigal son in Luke 15. Let us look again at this description of grace through the lens of our imaginations, as the prodigal son might have described his experience as the essence of God's love.

The Prodigal's Father as Example of God's Forgiveness

"I can't believe it. Seven years without a word. Seven years of no contact. But I'm getting ahead of myself. Let me start many years back. You see, my father is a farmer, and he was successful at it. He worked real hard at being a farmer, had a nice stretch of land and a good herd of stock as well. It wasn't a bad deal; it just wasn't what I wanted for myself.

"As I was growing up, my father taught my brother and me all about that farm. Everywhere dad farmed or fed the animals or cleaned up after them, we were there doing our part. If the fields needed to be tilled, we got out our short sleeves and tilled. If the fencing needed to be moved, we were there with our muscles and mallets. If the grain was low in the feed bins, we were there tearing open the sacks. If some animal . . . well, you get the picture. Not a great job, but it was OK. My father taught us some strong values, too—always work hard, always do what you know to be right, always do it as best as you can, and always spend mealtime with family. That is to say, never eat by yourself. He used to say it was a waste of good food and good company.

"Now when I was just a kid, I thought this was all the greatest—living on the farm, fresh air, wide-open spaces, the animals, and Mom's home cooking. Imagine how envious all the kids at school were. Everyone always wanted to come home with me. But as I got older, life on the farm began to lose some of its charm. I wasn't going anywhere. Dad wasn't either. At the end of everyday, he still had chores that needed to be done and the knowledge that tomorrow would be more of the same thing. I just felt like my brother and I were trapped in the same rut. If just one of us could break out, get away, make something of himself, or get to do all those things everyone else seemed to be doing.

"So, when I turned 18, I asked my dad for some of his savings so that I could go out and try to become something different. It was a frightful scene. He and I really had it out, and I said some things just to make him mad. He couldn't believe it or understand why I didn't want to stay with the farm. Dad loves the farm, and he always had looked forward to sharing in the farm with us in the future. It's OK, but I had to see what I was missing. I had to find myself. I had to have fun. Like I said, it was a frightful scene, worse than I figured it would be. At the end, my dad gave me what would have been my inheritance if I had waited until . . . well, anyway, he gave me cash. It was most of his savings. Of course, that left the property, the farm, for my brother to inherit. Dad was very sad. But I took the money, knowing once I got away I wouldn't be back.

"Well, I had my fun. I went everywhere and kicked up a storm. I had parties with friends, people I wanted to be my friends, and people I never even wanted to know. I went to school for one semester and only went to three classes. I got little silly part-time jobs and never tried once to do anything there. And no one cared. I tried fast foods, fast diets, fast women, and more. I went to ball games, bars, and the beach. I tried it all. I ran for city hall; I threw bottles through the windows of city hall and spent two weeks in the jail next to city hall. I ate more junk food, slept in more junkyards, and hung around with more junkies than you'd find at a rehab center. Now they didn't look like junkies, none of us did, but we were. I was having the time of my life. I was finding myself, or so I thought.

"One time, my big-time friends and I went to see a state fair. It was a wonderful treat! The specialties at the fair included big fat hogs, preserve tasting, biggest pumpkin contests, and even a squash shaped like a cow (complete with udder!). We just laughed and laughed. We made so much fun of what went on. I laughed so hard, I cried.

"Later I went home alone for dinner, and it all hit me. There I was eating in my apartment, sitting among the remains of an instant dinner, talking to myself. This was nothing new because I was the only one who listened to me anyway. I figured out I wasn't happy. I didn't like what I was doing, I didn't like where I was headed, and I didn't like myself. I'm not sure I even knew who I was. What was the big difference between cleaning up farm garbage and the kind of garbage I was sitting in? I'll tell you the difference. Others were with you at the farm. It dawned on me that I was better off at home with my dad and brother cleaning up after cows then living this charade with high society folk.

"Right then, I decided to go home. It had been seven years. Never once had I contacted my family to tell them where I was or what I was doing. I didn't even let them know I was coming back. I didn't want to give them time to think about how angry they were with me. I hitchhiked back and snuck in right at dusk. By coincidence, it was dinnertime. And you know what I found? There was my place setting all ready.

"Seven years without any contact and my dinner was sitting there ready. Night after night for seven years, without even a hint that I might be there, my dad and brother had dinner with my place ready. Seven years, no contact, and the place setting was ready. I couldn't believe it. It was like the only thing that had been missing was my own presence at the table. And whose choice was that?"

Overcoming Self-Defeating Life-Styles

The power of the story of the prodigal son is in our identification with the characters in the story and our longing to experience our relationships on the same level as this father and son. There is no evidence that the father had forgotten his disappointment with his younger son and the pain that he had experienced for seven years. It is evident from the Scriptures, that the older, more responsible son remembered every detail of his younger brother's behavior and needed to make sure that some accounting of the transgressions took place!

What is striking about the parable is that the father saw beyond the estrangement with his son and remembered a time when they had been close. The father remembered the hopes he had invested in both of his sons at their birth. He remembered the years of toiling hard in the fields to provide them with the opportunities of life and the security of a caring home. He never forgot the potential the younger boy had, in spite of his unscrupulous behavior. In the eyes of the father, forgiveness was possible because he continued to love the son for who he was and who he could become; he did not erase that vision in light of how the son had distorted his potential for seven years.

Jesus gave us the best description of how love overcomes fear in this parable. He described how infinite God's capacity is to see beyond our self-defeating efforts to control our destinies. Jesus reminded us that forgiveness is possible because God never loses the capacity to imagine us living at our potential, instead of stuck in the mire of our own self-centered idolatries.

To overcome the problem of self-defeating life-styles one must realize the spiritual truth of this parable about forgiveness. The issues and conflicts of one's journey cannot be glossed over and ignored. Sin is confronted as sin, and self-defeating strategies must be seen for their limitations. But strategies can be altered, and balance can be achieved through the media of love and empathy. *Agape* can be imparted in a significant measure through those who can see us through the eyes of imagination and affirm our creative potential, even in the midst of our chaotic past and present.

The New Testament drives home the concept of creative

personhood in its statements concerning abundant life, overcoming, and conquering. Jesus was very clear in His life, and in His words, that His intention is for each of His disciples to live the abundant life. Jesus said, "The thief comes only to steal and kill and destroy; I came that they may have life, and have it abundantly" (John 10:10). Jesus also said, "I have said this to you, that in me you may have peace. In the world you have tribulation; but be of good cheer, I have overcome the world" (John 16:33). The apostle Paul reminded us that love does overcome fear when he wrote:

> No, in all these things we are more than conquerors through him who loved us. For I am sure that neither death, nor life, nor angels, nor principalities, nor things present, nor things to come, nor powers, nor height, nor depth, nor anything else in all creation, will be able to separate us from the love of God in Christ Jesus our Lord (Rom. 8:37-39).

The truth of these passages enables us to have hope as we engage the self-defeating aspects of our life-styles. As we seek to find a new balance within the strategies that we use, we can be reminded that God through Christ has provided us with the encouragement to harness the destructive aspects of our anxiety. By the grace of God, we can restore our spirits to a state of harmony and peace with Him.